MALTA

BLUE GUIDE

MALTA

Edited by
PETER McGREGOR EADIE

With 10 Maps, and Plans

LONDON
ERNEST BENN LIMITED

RAND McNALLY & COMPANY
CHICAGO, NEW YORK, SAN FRANCISCO

FIRST EDITION 1968
SECOND EDITION 1979

Published by Ernest Benn Limited
25 New Street Square, London EC4A 3JA
& Sovereign Way, Tonbridge, Kent TN9 1RW

Rand McNally & Company
Chicago, New York, San Francisco

Photoset by Cold Composition Ltd.,
Tonbridge, Kent

Printed in Great Britain by Page Brothers (Norwich) Ltd.

ISBN *Library* 0 510 01614-6   528-84636-1 (USA)
ISBN *Paperback* 0 510 01615-4   528-84634-5 (USA)

PREFACE

The second edition of Blue Guide to Malta owes much to the original research of Stuart Rossiter who prepared the first edition eleven years ago in 1968, and I would like to thank him for his useful comments on the preparation of the new edition.

Since 1968, major political and economic changes have taken place. Malta and the Maltese islands became a Republic in 1974 and in March this year the last of the British forces withdrew. For centuries the Maltese have earned the major part of their income from servicing foreign armed forces and to replace this financial deficit they have planned ahead during the last decade to expand and improve their tourist resources. This has been a wise economic approach based on the knowledge that Malta has more hours of sunshine than any destination in the Mediterranean.

In 1968, the tourist arrivals in Malta were 138,000 and in 1978 the figure expected is 425,000 and during the decade between Malta has launched her own National Airline—Air Malta—which now serves some ten destinations in Europe, including London, Birmingham and Manchester. Most of the major cruise ships—Swan Hellenic, Karageorgis, Epirotiki etc, call in because the country is rich in historical treasures. Two new museums were inaugurated in 1974, the National Museum of Fine Arts in Valletta, the National Museum of Natural History in Mdina and more recently a War Museum was opened in Fort St. Elmo.

The earliest islanders quickly developed a skill in fashioning the limestone of which Malta is largely composed. The prehistoric temples are unique of their period alike for their topographical concentration, their complexity and their state of preservation. Largely unaltered stand the splendid fortifications of the Knights of St John, built at a period when Italian military engineering had absorbed the scientific principles and aesthetic feeling of the Renaissance. If these were generally designed by professionals from the mainland, their construction and the plans of the domestic buildings of the Order were usually entrusted to Maltese architects. Though their work derived broadly from the styles of Spain, France and Sicily, it shows also marked local characteristics: a long tradition had absorbed Siculo-Norman and Saracenic influences. Local craftmanship survived the colonial period, the military buildings of which, erected mostly in Victorian times, have a grace and strength more reminiscent of the 18C. With their deep arcading and often spectacular siting, they make a distinguished and harmonious contribution to the landscape. Thus, with its long history paramount at every step, Malta has a fascination very much its own.

The last decade has seen a growth in services and self catering accommodation in all grades and their attractive prices in relation to similar destinations have led them to be packaged by some sixty UK tour operators. Linked to the demand for accommodation has been a very substantial increase in outside restaurants and a growing interest in local dishes. Car hire is the cheapest in Europe and prices are government controlled. At the time of going to press the rates are about £4 per day. Most people who drive therefore hire. Non-drivers find that the bus services out of Valletta to all parts of the island are reliable, regular and cheap with the furthest destination not costing more than 12 pence.

There are no great distances to travel and every corner of the islands is accessible. Paradoxically, however, the concentration of population, the complexity of the road system, and the ubiquitous stone terrace walls make Malta very confusing while many unfamiliar constructions rouse the curiosity. The topography has therefore been described in rather greater detail than is usual in the Blue Guides, an attempt being made to satisfy the passing curiosity of the traveller as to identity and historical interest of prominent and unfamiliar buildings even where these may be of limited artistic merit or banal present use. The reader should not assume that every building mentioned is worthy of a diversion in its own right, and may justly be satisfied to ignore what is not emphasized by bold type.

Though the prehistoric monuments of Malta have been objects of wonder for more than a century, they have, until recently, been widely misunderstood. Many of the conclusions of earlier archaeologists have been reversed in the last ten years. Even the latest and most reliable general books can be misleading. For this reason *Professor John D. Evans* of the Institute of Archaeology in the University of London was asked expressly for this book to write the essay that here appears under his name.

The maps and plans are wholly the work of *Mr John Flower.* The information there presented, while based immediately on editorial observation, owes much to the excellent maps of the Directorate of Overseas Surveys and to Baron Iguanez' pioneer Street Guide, to both of which acknowledgement is here made.

The editor is indebted to *P. J. Camilleri* Director of the Malta Government Tourist Office, London; to *Joseph Mallia,* Chairman of the National Tourist Organisation of Malta and his staff and in particular *Edward Melillo* at the UK desk; to *Francis Mallia,* Director of Museums; to *Chevalier Joseph Gallea,* Archivist to the Knights of the Order of St John and to *Dr Vincent A. Despasquale,* Librarian of the Malta National Library. No guide can be written without assistance from colleagues working in the tourist industry who are able to provide from their files invaluable information and in this connection grateful thanks must go to *Eric Gerrada-Azzopardi* of Air Malta, *John Dixon* of Cadogan Travel, Gordon McNally of Exchange Travel, *Joseph Pisani* of the Corinthia Palace Hotel and *Anthony Buttigieg de Piro* of the Malta Hilton. Especial thanks also to *Mario Buhagiar* who kindly read through the completed text and made many useful suggestions and to *Fionnuala McGregor Eadie* for her invaluable help during all stages of preparation.

The Editor is well aware of the difficulty of avoiding errors, and suggestions for the correction or improvement of the Guide will be most gratefully welcomed.

CONTENTS

GOZO

MAPS AND PLANS

MAPS

PLANS

MALTA IN ANTIQUITY

by Professor J. D. EVANS

There is as yet no indication that the Maltese islands were inhabited by man during the Palaeolithic. The earliest known traces of human occupation are datable to about the beginning of the 5M B.C. They probably represent the remains left by a few boatloads of people, who at about this time ventured to cross the sixty odd miles of sea which separate Malta from Sicily, bringing with them some seed corn and domestic animals, to colonise and farm this still virgin territory. The islands are visible in clear weather from Cape Passero at the S.E. tip of Sicily (which had been inhabited since the later part of the Palaeolithic period), and the crossing itself would not have presented any special difficulties in good weather conditions. Thus, in an unspectacular way, Maltese history began, a history which has been unexpectedly rich and varied; for, small as they are, and virtually destitute of natural resources, the Maltese islands can boast of a past more fascinating in itself, and often much more significant in a wider historical context, than that of many larger and richer countries. At several periods, indeed, they have played a role of vital importance to the fates of empires and even of continents! Before all this came about, however, the early inhabitants of the islands created some very remarkable cultures of their own, which, though of strictly local significance, are still of the greatest interest.

The prehistory of Malta can be divided into three main sections, which are now called Neolithic, Copper Age and Bronze Age. There is no Iron Age division of the prehistoric period, since at the time the Phoenicians began to colonise the island group in the 8C B.C. the inhabitants seem still to have been using only bronze. The term Neolithic was originally applied by the great Maltese archaeologist, Sir Themistocles Zammit, to the period during which the spectacular megalithic temples were built, but when, in the early 1960s, Dr David Trump's excavations at Skorba (cf p. 10), brought to light evidence for a long period of human occupation which preceded these, the name was applied to this earliest stage. The period of the temples then became known as the Copper Age, not because any objects of this metal have actually been found in the buildings of that time, but simply because it is the term used to designate the same period of time in Sicily and Italy, where copper is sometimes found on the sites.

The dating of the prehistoric period in Malta before the beginning of the middle phase of the Bronze Age (Borġ in-Nadur culture) is based almost entirely on a number of radiocarbon determinations made on material found in various sites. The radiocarbon method of dating is now well known and widely accepted, and is in general use for periods back to about 50,000 B.C. A certain amount of the isotope C14 is present in all living organic matter; this decays at a known rate, and ceases to be replaced once the organism dies. In theory, therefore, it is a simple matter to calculate the age of organic material, such as charcoal, found

9

in an archaeological deposit, and so date the deposit itself. Unfortunately there are complications due to a number of factors, the most important of which is the variation at different times of the total amount of C14 in the atmosphere. This means that the dates produced by laboratories have to be calibrated to allow for these variations. There is not yet complete agreement about the calibration scale, and several systems are in use, but it is nevertheless possible to give approximate figures. When calibrated, the dates from Malta indicate that the Neolithic period began about 5000 B.C. and lasted for more than a millennium, while the Copper Age occupied most of the 4 and 3M B.C. There was a sharp cultural break at this point, though we do not know if there was also a gap in time, after which the Bronze Age began and lasted until the coming of the Phoenicians in the 8C B.C. (see Table, p. 30).

Within each of the three periods of Maltese prehistory a number of finer subdivisions can be recognized. These phases, which vary considerably in length, are characterized chiefly by changing pottery styles, but also to some extent by changes in other aspects of the material equipment. The individual phases are each named after an archaeological site where material of that type was first found, or where it is particularly well represented. The available C14 dates help in dating some of the phases, though there are some discrepancies and plenty of scope for argument about the dates for the beginning and end of individual phases and even, to a lesser extent, of the three main periods. Apart from this, some links with datable archaeological material in other areas are also helpful from time to time, especially in the dating of the Bronze Age phases.

NEOLITHIC

Three phases are now recognized within this period. These are known as the *Għar Dalam, Grey Skorba* and *Red Skorba* phases. Until the recent excavations carried out by Dr D. H. Trump at the Skorba site only the first of these was known. This, the *Għar Dalam* phase, still represents what seems, so far as we know, to be the earliest occupation of the islands. The characteristic pottery is very distinctive, being brown or greyish in colour and often decorated with elaborate patterns which were impressed or incised in the wet surface of the clay before the pot was fired. Both the shapes and decoration of this *Impressed Ware,* as it is called, show a remarkably close resemblance to those made and used by the earliest Neolithic inhabitants of Sicily. The similarity is so great that it is clear that the earliest inhabitants of the Maltese islands must have sailed across from Sicily. The pottery of the two succeeding Skorba phases seems to develop quite naturally out of this tradition, without any sign of a break in the continuity. Nevertheless, there were considerable changes which came about in the course of time, notably the loss of the rich and elaborate impressed decoration. In fact, very little decoration occurs on the pottery of either of the Skorba phases, and when it does it is very simple. The shapes tend to be more angular, and a kind of ladle or dipper with a broad handle whose top is shaped like an M is very characteristic of both phases. The *Grey Skorba* phase is so named because the pottery is normally grey in colour, while during the

Red Skorba phase a very striking red monochrome surface was developed.

The type site of the Għar Dalam phase is a natural cave, where there was found, in addition to the archaeological material, which was confined to the upper levels, a great mass of animal bones, including those of animals long extinct in the Maltese islands, such as elephant and hippopotamus, as well as red deer. These had been washed into the cave long before man appeared on the islands. Some human teeth also found here, which exhibit an abnormality which is fairly characteristic of those of Neanderthal man, seemed to suggest the presence of a group of Palaeolithic hunters until it was realized that the later prehistoric population of Malta had teeth which also exhibited this peculiarity fairly frequently.

It is uncertain whether the people who left their impressed pottery and flint implements at Għar Dalam used the cave to live in or simply for burying their dead, or perhaps for both purposes. The cave was also used by later people who seem to have disturbed the deposits left by the earliest people, so making it difficult to judge. Other caves occupied during the Għar Dalam phase are also known, but sherds of this pottery have also turned up from time to time on the sites of some of the megalithic temples. Probably these came from settlements in the open on sites later occupied by religious monuments, but it was not until the excavation of the Skorba site that the first remains of a village of this phase were brought to light. Part of an oval hut dating to the Għar Dalam phase was found here, the foundations being of rough stones, the superstructure probably of wattle and daub or mud brick. A portion of a more massive wall, which ran in a straight line for a length of sixteen feet was also dated to this phase, though its purpose was not at all clear. The Skorba village continued to be inhabited through the following two phases, to which the site has been given its name, but the chief architectural feature which has been uncovered belongs to the Red Skorba phase. This consists of two separate oval rooms, measuring about 26 ft by just over 17 ft, and constructed in very much the same way as the hut just described. However, these buildings do not seem to have been ordinary dwellings; the contents included a number of remarkable stylized figurines of clay representing female human figures, some goat skulls with horns attached, and some cow toe bones which had been rubbed down at one end to enable them to be set upright. This curious material suggests that they were probably shrines of some kind rather than ordinary domestic huts.

With regard to the way the Neolithic people disposed of their dead we are not well informed. As already noted, some of the human bones found in Għar Dalam may represent the remains of burials of this period, but it is impossible to be certain. A few fragments of human bone were found in the Skorba village, but they were not in any sense burials, and no other evidence is available.

The Neolithic people of Malta were farmers who had a long tradition of food-production behind them already when they arrived. Two pottery heads of what are probably sheep were found at Għar Dalam. They are of the characteristic grey fabric and may be parts of elaborate handles. Bones of sheep or goat, cow, pig and dog were found in the Għar Dalam levels at Skorba, and carbonized grains of barley, wheat and lentils were also found in them. A quern (or simple millstone) for grinding the grain was also found. Farming probably supplied the greater part of the food these early people ate, but they may well have varied their diet by collecting shell-fish (pierced shells were used as ornaments). The finding at Skorba of slingstones also suggests that they did a little hunting of whatever wild animals and birds were available.

From the first occupation of the Maltese islands by man it was necessary to import certain essential materials which were not to be found there. At this time stone was the only material known which provided effective cutting tools. Though local chert was available from which rough implements could be made, it was found worth while to import supplies of good flint from Sicily. Another material, obsidian, which is a natural glass found in volcanic deposits, makes superlatively sharp knives. It is of relatively rare occurrence, and was much prized and widely traded by Neolithic people. The Neolithic inhabitants of Malta and Gozo were obtaining supplies of this material from two different sources, the Lipari (or Aeolian) Islands, to the North of Sicily, and the island of Pantelleria to the w. The two types of obsidian have a distinctive appearance, but the provenance has also been confirmed by spectrographic analysis. The Lipari Islands were the more important source of the material, and as the period went on they, with their highly organized commerce, became the main suppliers of the Maltese islands. Lava was also imported into the islands, presumably from the area of Etna in Sicily, probably for making such things as querns. A small axe-shaped pendant of a green igneous stone found at Skorba must also have been imported.

Though the development of the pottery from the Għar Dalam to the Red Skorba phase seems to be a local one, it is noticeable that the red monochrome finish of the Red Skorba pottery is well matched in the Diana pottery of the Final Neolithic in the Lipari Islands and Sicily, and very similar lugs with expanded ends are found on both types. It seems likely that such convergence resulted from the close trading links between these areas. The Red Skorba phase is dated by radiocarbon in Malta to the first half of the 4M B.C., and a similar date for the Diana type of pottery is well supported by a good deal of evidence.

COPPER AGE

The beginning of this period is marked by what appears to be a sharp break in the continuity of the cultural tradition in Malta. A new kind of pottery, the Żebbuġ ware, came into use, which is strikingly different from any of the Neolithic styles. For the first time, too, there is evidence that the dead were being buried collectively in artificially constructed tombs. It almost seems as though a new people had arrived to replace the earlier inhabitants, so complete is the change. Of course, archaeological evidence can sometimes be misleading in these matters, since fashions and customs can change without a change of population; but at all events the culture of the inhabitants of the Maltese islands took a completely new direction at this point, a direction which it continued to follow steadily for the next thousand years, and which eventually culminated in the construction and adornment of the great megalithic temples which are so famous throughout the world.

Five distinct phases can be recognized during the period, each characterized by distinct pottery style, though as in the Neolithic period an overall continuity of development can be discerned throughout. The stages are known as the *Zebbuġ, Mġarr, Ġgantija, Saflieni* and *Tarxien* phases.

The **Pottery** of the first of these is of two kinds, a dark mottled fabric, and a much lighter yellowish kind. Both kinds are decorated with lines deeply cut or incised into the surface of the clay, which were filled with a white or red paste to make them stand out. The most striking vases are jars with pear-shaped bodies and bell-like necks, which are sometimes decorated in a way which seems to show that they suggested human figures to their makers. This pottery is most closely similar to wares in use in Sicily at the beginning of the Copper Age there, and it may be that Sicilian influence was involved in its development.

The pottery of the *Mġarr* phase in Malta took the Zebbuġ type of decoration a stage further, substituting broad cut-out bands for the deep, narrow lines of the Zebbuġ style. The shapes, however, are simpler than in the earlier period.

In the following *Ġgantija* phase there was a further, and rather unexpected, development in the pottery decoration. The patterns were now made by scratching lines on the surface of the pot after it had been fired. Parts of these designs were hatched in the same technique, and finally an incrustation of red ochre was applied to the scratched lines and the hatched areas. The effect produced was that of a coloured pattern, the scratched lines being invisible on the finished product. The patterns are generally curvilinear, a favourite *motif* being two converging lines with a little circle at the point where they meet; it looks rather like a schematic representation of a comet with its tail of fire, though it is probably completely abstract. One kind of near-globular vase has the upper part entirely covered with a chequer-board pattern of squares, alternately left plain and filled with some kind of hatching or other decoration, while the lower part has the more common 'comet' type of decoration. The shapes of the pots are mostly rounded and rather baggy in this phase. As will be seen later, the Ġgantija phase was an important one and probably lasted a long time.

The *Saflieni* phase, on the other hand, seems to have been a short one. It has only been certainly identified as a separate chronological phase in the last few years, and it is still not very well known. The pottery is mostly in the Ġgantija tradition, though some new shapes, and even some new types of decoration appear. The scratched decoration continues, with both free curvilinear and chequer-board patterns, and is covered with red ochre as before. Some vases, however, have a surface which has been roughened by jabbing the wet clay all over with a bone point. The most striking new shapes are a flat based dish and a more or less biconical vessel known as the 'Saflieni' bowl. This is made in a wide variety of sizes. There are some extremely large, as well as some very miniaturized, examples. They are often elaborately decorated.

The final phase of the Copper Age is known as the *Tarxien* phase, and is named after the most elaborate of the temple-complexes, which belongs largely to this phase. The characteristic pottery is much more varied than that of any of the earlier ones. The standard decoration is still by scratched lines covered with red incrustation, but the patterns are different and much more elegant. They are usually based on a graceful volute *motif* and frequently recall the ornamental patterns popular in Middle Minoan Crete. Besides this, however, a whole range of new, and often elaborate techniques is used in the decoration of some of the pottery. These range from the use of applied studs or raised lumps set in a background of white paste inlay, to a kind of applied scale decoration which was used on large storage vessels. The forms of the pots in this phase tend to be angular, and frequently give the impression of being imitated from metal vessels, of which, however, no trace has yet been found in Malta. The Tarxien phase may have lasted a fairly long time, probably coming to a close fairly early in the 2M B.C. It represents the highest point of the Copper Age civilization of the Maltese islands.

Almost all our evidence concerning the Maltese people of the Copper Age comes from their **Tombs and Temples.** Until the excavation of the Skorba site nothing at all was known about their settlements, and this still remains the only village site of this period which has been located. Remains of huts of the Zebbuġ, Mġarr and Ġgantija phases were found at Skorba, which were all much the same in construction as the Neolithic ones. In shape they differed slightly, tending more towards the sub-rectangular. The floors were of beaten earth or *torba* (a plaster made of crushed limestone); the walls had stone footings, surmounted by mud brick and wattle and daub superstructures. Quernstones, and other remains suggestive of domestic activities, were found in them. In contrast to this scanty data about the everyday life of the people stands the great mass of evidence about their religious and funerary customs, though it is a pity that so much of this comes from important sites, including several of the most important temples, which were excavated (or rather cleared), before archaeology had developed as a science. Much evidence was destroyed in this early work, and many objects which were preserved are virtually without context.

The custom of burying the dead in collective tombs certainly goes back to the beginning of this period. It is illustrated by a group of five tombs which were accidentally discovered near the village of Zebbuġ. The Zebbuġ phase was named after this group of tombs. When found, they were shallow oval pits in the rock which contained numbers of broken and disarticulated human and animal bones, together with sherds of pottery, flint tools and bone and shell ornaments. In one there was also a roughly carved human head which had perhaps formed part of a statue or a gravestone. It is possible that these tombs had once been real chamber tombs, but had been partially destroyed later by minor quarrying operations of the kind that have always gone on in Malta. Some complete jars of the Zebbuġ style which survive in the National Museum and in private collections are most likely to have survived in tombs of this kind, though we know nothing for certain about where they came from. Such small chamber tombs, entered from a small circular pit, are known for certain to have been in use during the following, Mġarr, phase. Potsherds of this type were found in some of the tombs of a well-known group on the Xemxija Heights, above the N.W. side of St Paul's Bay, though most of the pottery found there dated from the Ġgantija and Tarxien phases.

It is clear that collective tombs of this simple kind were in use in Malta and Gozo throughout the Copper Age. In at least one instance, however, a much more elaborate kind of rock-cut burial place was constructed (or perhaps one might better say it evolved) over a long period of time. This is the famous Hal Saflieni Hypogeum, which consists of a remarkable agglomeration of halls and chambers cut out of the soft globigerina limestone. It seems to have contained the remains of not less than 6000 people, together with the grave-goods buried with them and probably some other material. Some of the smaller chambers which form a part of this strange monument are very much like single rock tombs of the type found at Xemxija, though generally larger and more carefully finished. The larger chambers and the great halls have a quite different character; they are richly adorned with painting and carving, the latter intended to reproduce underground the characteristics of the architecture of the megalithic temples. They are ceremonial, if not public, places. The germ of the development which produced Hal Saflieni is, however, to be seen at Xemxija, where two of the tombs are set side by side, and intercommunicate, though each has also its separate entrance. Pottery of all the Copper Age styles was found at Hal Saflieni, and this indicates how long its construction must have taken, since the carved halls imitate features of the temples erected in the later Ġgantija and Tarxien phases, while some of the painted ceilings resemble the decoration which first appears on pottery in the Tarxien phase.

Collective burial in rock-cut tombs is a fairly common kind of funerary custom around the shores of the Mediterranean, but the great megalithic temples of Malta and Gozo are unique. True, megalithic monuments are found in many other parts of the West Mediterranean and elsewhere in Western Europe, but they are normally communal graves, like the rock-tombs, not temples. So far as we know, none of the Maltese megalithic monuments were ever used for burial, though they were the locus of an elaborate cult which was evidently very closely linked with the ancestors buried in the rock-tombs and the Hal Saflieni Hypogeum. It is even likely that the peculiar form of the temples, based on clusters of semicircular or horseshoe-shaped rooms, derives ultimately from the form of some of the burial chambers. The largest of the tombs at Xemxija, Tomb 5, has a curious lobed plan, which seems to have been dictated by the necessity of leaving portions of rock standing in order to support the roof, which might otherwise have collapsed. These divided the rear part of the room into a chamber of curved spaces. This plan is very similar to that of the most primitive of the surviving shrines, the smaller of the two buildings which make up the temple at Ta Ħaġrat (Mġarr), though there was no functional necessity for such a plan.

Though the temples were not used for burial, the Hypogeum was certainly used for some sort of religious purposes and this provides some further evidence for the complex links between the tombs and the temples. There may even have been a megalithic building in front of the original entrance to the Hypogeum. However, none of the surviving temples can be shown to date from the earlier phases of the Copper Age. They seem all to have been built, or at least to have reached their present form, in the Ġgantija and later phases. Like the Hypogeum, however, the Maltese temples were complex structures which were subject to periodic alteration, rebuilding and extension over a long period of time.

This piecemeal construction often makes if difficult for us to trace their full history. A good analogy is the complicated architectural history of many European churches and cathedrals.

Most of the temple-complexes consist of one or more separate 'units', each having its own entrance which leads into a group of three or more rooms arranged around one or more square or rectangular courts, though a few are more irregular structures. In form and technique of building the most primitive of the surviving monuments are the two known as Ta Ħaġrat in the village of Mġarr. As already mentioned, the smaller of these, built of rough stones, has a plan which is reminiscent of a large rock-cut tomb. The bigger building marks a considerable advance on this. In plan it is trefoil-shaped, having three separate chambers all opening off a rectangular paved court. Two of these are roughly circular, while the third is really a kind of irregular space off which opens the entrance to the smaller building. The entrance to the larger building, which serves also as the entrance to the whole monument, is set in the centre of a concave façade, a feature which is found in megalithic architecture in various parts of western Europe. The whole building is surrounded by an outer wall, between which and the chambers inside is a packing of earth and stones. This building is in essence the model for all the later temples.

A very similar trefoil temple can be seen in the Kordin III complex, though it seems a little more developed in that, instead of the circular chambers, there are semicircular rooms which are fenced off from the central court by stone partitions. This building shares a common façade with one which looks rather like a throw-back to a much earlier type, since it has a rather indeterminate lobed plan. The next development is illustrated by the massive monument appropriately known as the Ġgantija, situated near the village of Xagħra, in Gozo. Here two 'units' stand side by side, sharing a common façade. Each of them has five rooms instead of three, and they are arranged round two courts joined by a short corridor. There are, however, some significant differences between these two 'units', and the southernmost seems to be the earlier. Its three rear rooms, arranged in the usual trefoil pattern, are much larger than the two front ones, which is the opposite of what is normally found in units with five or more rooms. It almost seems as though the front rooms were added here as an afterthought.

The northern 'unit', on the other hand, has a more orthodox plan. The two rooms which lie on either side of the first court are larger than those at the back, while the rear room, which faces the entrance, has begun to shrink in size; it is already quite small and is filled up by a kind of niche built of slabs. Excavations have shown that these two 'units' were both erected during the Ġgantija phase, though the niche in the northern one seems to have been added during the Tarxien phase.

Apart from one example in the Tarxien complex, the 'units' which go to make up the later temple-complexes mostly resemble the northern building of the Ġgantija pair very closely in plan, save that the old rear room was even further reduced in size, so that it is only just big enough to accommodate a small niche. The exception is the central building of the main group at Tarxien, which has three pairs of lateral semicircular chambers, instead of the usual two. This may be partly, if not entirely, explained by the necessity of filling the space between the other two buildings, and the first pair of rooms are really more like an oval court. A wholly exceptional complex is the main group of buildings at Ħaġar Qim, where we seem to have the remains of one orthodox 'unit', which has, however, been altered so as to have an entrance at the back as well as the front, while on the w. side of it there has grown up a very irregular complex of oval rooms. This complex seems to have been entirely constructed during the Ġgantija phase, but it does not fit into any scheme of development.

The megalithic buildings show evidence of the progressive development in the skill and ambition of their builders. The early ones, like those at Ta Ħaġrat, are constructed of rough boulders and slabs of coralline limestone. This technique of construction is also seen, on a much larger scale, in both the Ġgantija buildings, though here dressed blocks and slabs of the softer globigerina limestone were also used in certain places, while the outer casing was made of huge slabs of coralline limestone, surmounted by courses of blocks. The walls of the rooms were originally finished by covering them with a mass of clay, capped with a coat of lime plaster which was painted red. Traces of this covering have been found adhering to the walls at some points. In later buildings upright slabs surmounted by coursed blocks were used for the construction of both inner and outer walls. The harder coralline limestone was still preferred for the outer casing, but for the interior the softer globigerina limestone, which could be cut and dressed exactly to shape was used. There is no evidence that plaster was used to surface the walls of these later temples, and indeed none would be needed, so fine is the finish and the fitting of the slabs.

Even in the most primitive of the surviving monuments the walls of the chambers, in so far as they survive, show signs of curving inwards to form some sort of vault. In the later buildings the slabs which form the lower part of the walls often lean slightly inwards, while the courses of dressed blocks which surmounted them were corbelled. Each course slightly overlapped the one below, thus gradually reducing the total space to be roofed. Some of the smaller monuments might have been roofed entirely with stone in this way, or by finishing off with a stone slab or slabs at a certain height. But the Maltese building stone will not span a space of more than about 2 m without intermediate support. There is no evidence of the existence of such supports in the larger temples, and it seems quite impossible that their rooms can have been roofed in this manner. Moreover, traces of the huge slabs employed would surely have been found. So either they were open to the sky, in which case the courses of carefully corbelled blocks seem a curiously elaborate waste of labour, or else they were roofed with some perishable material, such as wood. This solution seems to be supported by the marks of a fierce conflagration which can be seen on the walls of some of the buildings at Tarxien, and also by the remarkably good state of preservation of some of the delicate carvings found there and in other temples, which seems surprising if they were exposed to the elements.

The pattern of occurrence of these carved blocks is interesting in itself. None are found in the remains of the Ta Ħaġrat or Kordin III monuments, or in other buildings which seem to belong to early stages on the development of the temples. There are a few in the South building at the Ġgantija and at Ħaġar Qim, but even these could well have been added after the original construction of the monuments. They are not an integral part of the construction, and some of them feature spiral patterns which seem appropriate only to the Tarxien phase. The earliest decoration employed was probably a sort of honeycomb pattern produced by pitting or drilling the surface. Some of the blocks originally decorated in this way were re-used later to carry spiral patterns, but occasionally some of the original pitting survives.

These amazing constructions were quite clearly temples, in the sense of being designed especially for the celebration of a cult. This seems to have become more and more elaborate as time went on, necessitating corresponding elaboration of the plan of the temples. As already suggested, the cult seems to have been closely connected with the dead, but it also involved at least one divine being, represented as a preter-naturally fat, but sexless, figure in the numerous statuettes and figurines which have been found. These figures are generally naked, but some are clothed from the waist down in a full, fringed skirt which reaches to the calves.

Animal sacrifices obviously played a large part in the worship which took place in the temples. The five-roomed 'units' of the later ones are always equipped with a pair of altar-like constructions which flank the entrance to the corridor that leads from the front to the rear rooms. The right-hand altar of such a pair in the s.w. 'unit' of the Tarxien complex, which is elaborately decorated with spiral patterns in relief, proved to be hollow. The interior was found to be filled with the burnt bones of sacrificed animals, while behind a neat stone plug which covered an opening in the front of the altar lay a curved stone knife, obviously the sacrificial instrument, reposing just where it had been carefully replaced after the last sacrifice. Numerous small cupboards and niches of stone slabs which have been found in various parts of the temples were usually full of burnt animal bones when found. Sheep, goat, pig and cow were all sacrificed, and in the Tarxien temples there were lively carvings of all of them on slabs and blocks found in various parts of the temples. To judge by some rough drawings on potsherds and a small stone head, snakes also played some part, though perhaps only a minor one. Circular holes pierced through some of the paving and threshold slabs into the ground below may have had to do with drink offerings, and in this connection it is interesting to note that thousands of fragments of a special type of handled bowl have been found in all the temples. Could they have been the ones which were used for the libations and then ceremoniously broken?

Such an elaborate religion is likely to have been highly organized, and almost certainly it had its priestly caste, whether these were full time officials or not. Traces of the existence of such an order have been found at Tarxien. There a large part of the middle temple 'unit' is separated off by a slab set up on edge, blocking the corridor which leads to the second and third sets of rooms. This slab is carved with a double spiral design which may symbolize a pair of watchful eyes which were intended to ward off the profane. A staircase led to an elevated corridor which ran behind the walls of these rooms. Originally there was doubtless a special entrance to them from this, but that part of the building has suffered much destruction and the evidence has been obliterated.

In two of the temple complexes, Tarxien and Mnajdra, small rooms have been discovered between the inner and outer walls. These were entered from the exterior and communicated with the temple only by means of a small rectangular opening in one of the wall slabs. They have been, no doubt correctly, interpreted as arrangements for the delivery of an oracle or some other kind of priestly mystification. At Tarxien remains of some clay figures were found which represented full-bodied men clothed from the waist down in elaborate pleated skirts which reached to their feet. Two of these have well-modelled heads with strongly marked features which may be portraits. It has been suggested that they represent priests of the cult. In the Hal Saflieni Hypogeum, which, as already noted, was used for certain religious and ceremonial purposes as well as for burial, two small models representing women, also clothed in decorated skirts, and reclining on well-modelled beds, were found. These odd finds may show us something which actually happened there, since we know that in Classical times sleeping in caves or other sacred places in order to obtain prophetic dreams—incubation, as it is called—was a familiar occurrence, in which priestesses were often involved.

In some of the temples at least there may have been a healing cult, as well as the main one connected with the dead and the divine figure. A number of figurines have been found apparently showing people suffering from a variety of ailments, as well as models of individual human limbs. It is all very reminiscent of the *ex votos* found in Classical sanctuaries, or still to be seen in Christian churches, especially in Mediterranean lands.

Though they give us a vivid picture of a society dominated by a religion to whose service it could and did divert an enormous amount of time and labour, the temples and tombs tell us very little about the more mundane side of life in Malta at this period. The sheer organization necessary for the planning and erection of the temples, and the evidence for the existence of priests and perhaps priestesses, suggest some degree of social complexity. The stone carvers, modellers and sculptors employed in the construction and adornment of the temples may well have been specialist craftsmen living off the produce of the farming community, as would also the priests themselves. The models of buildings or parts of buildings which have been found in several of the temples, together with the curious fragment of what seems to be a plan of a building (not a temple, but one with rectangular rooms) which was found at Tarxien, might even suggest that there were specialist architects. Recent study of the human bones found in the Xemxija tombs takes us even further. These bones are those of lightly built people with little muscular development, such as might be expected to come from regular manual work. It does not seem possible, therefore, that these can be the people who actually built the temples, or even tilled the fields. Perhaps burial in the rock tombs or the Hypogeum was reserved for members of a specially privileged class, and in this case the temple worship may have been for their benefit too.

Despite the use of the term Copper Age for this period of Maltese prehistory there is no evidence at present of the use of metal tools of any kind in the Maltese islands at this time. It would still be rash to conclude that they did not know of such things. A taboo on the use of metal objects in the temples is quite feasible, and we still know too little about the settlements to be sure what went on there. For the moment, however, the justification of the term Copper Age as applied to this period is simply that of convenience.

The chief tools employed in the construction of the monuments of this period were antler picks or wedges, which were used in conjunction with heavy stone mallets. These were used for hewing the rock in the Hypogeum, and probably also for the quarrying and rough shaping of the slabs for the temples. For the finer dressing, and probably also for carving, flint or obsidian blades would have been employed. The heavy slabs for the temples were moved by means of heavy balls of limestone which acted like ball-bearings, and of which many have been found on the temple sites. Ropes, which of course have not survived, were no doubt employed in conjunction with these. The slabs were raised into position with the aid of levers, probably wooden, for which sockets can still be seen on some of them.

Pendants of hard green stone in the shape of miniature axes are common finds, though real stone axes seem to have been extremely rare. But so are the stone mallets, and once more perhaps the situation would be different if we knew more settlement sites. Scrapers of flint and chert may have been used as wood planes, though they were no doubt also employed for skin dressing. Apart from scrapers, the most common flint and obsidian tools are knives, of which some very fine examples are known. The only weapons were biconical limestone slingstones (if that is really what they are), which may have been used in hunting.

A flourishing weaving industry is attested by finds of clay spindle-whorls, as well as by the models of figures clothed in elaborate skirts. It is possible that fine textiles may have been exported to pay for some of the materials which the Maltese had to obtain abroad, such as flint and obsidian (the former from Sicily, as before, the latter now exclusively from Lipari), lava for querns and igneous stone for axes, axe-pendants, etc. All these imported raw materials probably came from relatively near at hand, from Sicily, from other Italian islands or from the mainland itself. However, there is some evidence for wider contacts, particularly in the second half of the Maltese Copper Age. There are striking resemblances between Maltese pottery of the Tarxien phase and the contemporary Copper Age culture of Sardinia, the Ozieri culture, while both the Maltese and Sardinian cultures produced figurines which closely resemble types developed in the Cyclades and widely traded in the Aegean area during the 3M B.C.

BRONZE AGE

The great era of Maltese prehistory came to an end with the close of the Copper Age, and from one point of view everything else seems to be anticlimax. The Hypogeum and the great temples went out of use, and the highly developed art disappeared. The Bronze Age cultures have their own fascination, but they produced nothing comparable with the artistic and architectural achievement of the Copper Age. The Maltese Bronze Age can be divided into three main phases, but unlike those of the Neolithic and Copper Age they do not represent the continuous development of a single tradition, but rather a series of separate colonizations of the islands by people who came from elsewhere.

The first of these intrusive cultures is that of the *Tarxien Cemetery* people, so named after the large cremation cemetery which was the first site of this culture found. It was discovered by Sir T. Zammit in the course of his excavation of the Tarxien temples in 1915, and it is still by far the richest and most important one known. What happened to the flourishing Copper Age population is unknown, but it is clear that when the cemetery was formed at Tarxien the temples had gone out of use. If the tombs and temples were erected for the benefit of a privileged and powerful minority, then their abandonment need not mean a complete change of population, merely the replacement of the old oligarchs by new rulers. But whether numerous or not, the new people had completely different customs and equipment. Their cemetery consisted of a large number of cremations which were placed in large urns together with remains of clothing, ornaments, tools, weapons and pottery. A level platform had first been created by covering the floors of the old building with sand to a depth of about three feet, and it was on this that the material was found. Signs of burning over the whole area indicated that the cremation of the bodies (which was usually very imperfect) may have taken place on the spot, perhaps using old timbers from the roofing of the temples.

The objects found with the burials were numerous. Especially so were pots, of which over 200 complete examples were found. Many were decorated with incized, white-filled lines which formed rectilinear geometric patterns. Fragments of a loosely-woven fabric, probably originally dyed, were found, but these were not large enough to give any idea of the kind of garments worn. Beads and pendants of stone, ostrich-shell, faience, clay and even fish-vertebrae were present in large numbers.

A series of stylized clay figurines representing female figures seated on stools was found. Most of these are so schematized that it would be difficult to know what they were but for two more detailed and lifelike examples which are quite recognizably female human figures, though still very stylized. Both are wearing an elaborate headdress. Metal objects occur for the first time in Malta. Copper awls set in bone handles and probably also some copper axes were tools, but a series of triangular copper daggers which were found were quite possibly weapons. The bow was certainly in use as a weapon at this time, as shown by a few obsidian arrow-heads. These come from various sites, but probably all belong to the Tarxien Cemetery people, who seem to have been quite distinctly more warlike than previous inhabitants of Malta.

Though the characteristic pottery of the Tarxien Cemetery people has been found on a number of sites in Malta and Gozo (including the Skorba temples), most of the known material is still from the Tarxien site. The only monuments which they can be shown to have built themselves are some small and very rough structures, usually called 'dolmens', of which a number are known on both Malta and Gozo. They consist of a rough slab of coralline limestone between three and ten feet in length, which is supported a little above ground level by a series of slabs on edge or of pillars composed of several small blocks. Sometimes the capstone has a hole pierced vertically through it, and in one or two instances grooves are also to be seen on the upper surface. The rock below the capstone has sometimes been hollowed out to increase the height of the chamber. There is no trace in any instance of a mound which might have covered these structures, and most now stand on bare rock. One of them, situated at Ta Hammut, did however contain a little soil, which, when excavated, yielded some sherds of the typical pottery. A curious trapezoidal cairn at Wied Moqbol on the s. coast also produced some sherds of Tarxien Cemetery type. No human bones were found in either of these monuments but it is possible that they may have originally contained cremation burials.

The characteristic pottery of the Tarxien Cemetery people is similar in many ways to the pottery used by the contemporary Early Bronze Age people of the Lipari Islands. Pottery almost identical with the Tarxien Cemetery wares has been found at the site of Ognina just s. of Syracuse in Sicily. A little further afield, in the area around Otranto in the heel of Italy, there is some puzzling evidence of links with Malta in the form of a series of dolmens which closely resemble the Maltese ones, even in details such as perforated and grooved capstones. Unfortunately no pottery or other material has been found associated with any of them. Significant resemblances to the Tarxien Cemetery, Ognina and Lipari Early Bronze Age materials have been noted in the pottery used by people living in s. and w. Greece in the late 3 and early 2M B.C. The contemporary painted pottery of the Sicilian Castelluccio culture also displays many similarities to a painted ware in use in the Aegean during this period. Some strange pieces of bone decorated with bosses, and sometimes also incised decoration were found at Troy and at Lerna in the Peloponnese which resemble others which are known from the Castelluccio culture. A fragment of one was also found at Tarxien in Malta and probably belongs to the Tarxien Cemetery culture. These facts indicate a complex network of links between various Aegean and C. Mediterranean cultures of this period, but it is still difficult to be very precise about what they mean in human terms.

The fate of the Tarxien Cemetery people is as problematic as their origin. All that can be said for certain is that in the later 2M B.C. we find the Maltese islands in the hands of people who were using a new kind of equipment, but it may be that once more this betokens a change in the ruling group rather than in the mass of the population. The new culture takes its name from *Borġ in-Nadur*, which is the site of a settlement of the period situated close to St George's Bay in the Marsaxlokk. It occupies a triangular area of land between two converging *wieds* (or dry torrent beds). On two sides these valleys seem to have been thought to offer sufficient protection, but on the third side are the remains of a huge defensive wall with a massive central redoubt. Though it has not been possible to investigate the area of the settlement on a large scale, some oval huts with stone foundations have been located in the part just behind the defensive wall. In the s. corner of the triangular space delimited by the wall are the remains of a Copper Age temple-complex. When this was excavated in the 1920s it became clear that the ruins had been used in the Borġ in-Nadur phase for domestic purposes. Probably, then, the settlement was a large one, occupying more or less the whole of the space available, Recent excavations just behind the defensive wall have shown that the site may also have been occupied as a settlement already in the Tarxien Cemetery phase. A number of other settlements of the Borġ in-Nadur phase are known in Malta and Gozo, invariably sited on hilltops or other high and easily defensible ground. Some of them also have remains of defensive walls, though none on such a scale as that of Borġ in-Nadur itself.

The typical Borġ in-Nadur pottery has a shiny red surface which, however, flakes off easily to reveal a buff-coloured fabric below. Decoration is by deeply cut lines which have a square section, as though cut by a small chisel. They form simple but highly individual patterns which were filled with white paste. On some pots the red slip was used to make rough patterns instead of being applied all over. Shapes are two-handled bowls or cups which are often set on a high conical foot, high-handled bowls, cups and jugs, footed lamps, and small vases with elaborate T-shaped or axe-shaped handles. A very peculiar vessel is a rectangular basin with internal divisions, a characteristic also found occasionally in the very different Tarxien Cemetery ware.

Identical pottery has been found in the rock-cut tombs of certain cemeteries in the Syracuse district of Sicily, where it is associated with the local grey pottery, but also with Mycenaean pottery of the 14C B.C. Though these vases may well be imports from Malta, it seems evident that the tradition of potting which produced the Borġ in-Nadur wares originally stems from Sicily, where a tradition of red-slipped wares began in the Copper Age, in which period also similar divided basins are found. A single sherd of Mycenaean pottery datable to the 13C B.C. was found at Borġ in-Nadur, and what is possibly a second one was found in the recent Italian excavations at Tas Silġ.

A great many of the bell-shaped pits which are to be found cut into the rock all over Malta and Gozo may well date from the Borġ in-Nadur phase. Numbers of them occur near the settlements of this period and some have been found to contain the characteristic pottery. They were used doubtless for storing water and grain. Many others are probably later in date, since this kind of cistern or silo was in use in Malta at all later periods. The mysterious 'cart-tracks' (which in reality were probably ruts made by slide-cars, not wheeled vehicles) may also belong to this period. Some of them are to be found quite near the settlements of the Borġ in-Nadur people.

Apart from their agricultural activities the Borġ in-Nadur people carried on a busy weaving industry, as shown by the numerous spindle and loom weights of clay which have been found in their settlements. The curious clay anchor-shaped objects also found may well have been used in connection with some process of this industry, too. Small fragments of bronze, and a mould for making a bronze ornament found at Borg in-Nadur show that by now at any rate metal working was taking place on the islands. But finds of metal are still rare, which is not surprising, since it must still have been a costly imported material, not lightly to be discarded when it could be so easily re-used. No doubt old and broken metal objects were carefully collected and melted down by the smiths.

The Borġ in-Nadur culture survived for a long time in Malta. Recent work has made it possible to recognize three chronological subdivisions, each characterized by changes in the pottery. The final phase seems to have lasted down to about 800 B.C., or in other words to the end of the true prehistoric period. Thus the last of the three groups of intrusive Bronze Age people do not represent a separate chronological phase, but were contemporary with the late Borġ in-Nadur people. This group is known as the *Baħrija* culture, taking its name from a settlement site in the s.w. of Malta which seems in fact to be the only centre of this culture. Even at this site some of the pottery is clearly of Borġ in-Nadur type, and recent excavation work there has shown that it was originally a settlement of the Borġ in-Nadur people.

The typical Baħrija pottery has a black or grey surface. Some of it is nevertheless obviously derived from the Borġ in-Nadur tradition. The decoration is in the old 'chiselled' style, but includes the use of chipcarving (originally a technique used for decorating wooden vessels) and of patterns such as maeanders which were not known to the Borġ in-Nadur potters. Other vases, notably a series of angular bowls, are obviously foreign to Maltese tradition, though they have the same kind of decoration as the rest. There are also sherds of a new kind of painted ware.

The new decorative features and shapes point very clearly to the arrival of people coming from some part of South Italy. Presumably this was just a small group of immigrants who settled at the Baħrija site, where they succeeded in transforming the culture of the local inhabitants to some extent. Several objects found at Baħrija seem to confirm that the immigrants were of South Italian origin, such as fragments of rough pottery 'cheese-strainers', well known in South Italy, where pastoral activities had long been of paramount importance. A decorated clay weight, possibly a very large loom-weight, also has exact parallels in Calabria.

That the Baħrija people had contacts with the Borġ in-Nadur inhabitants of the other settlements is clearly shown by the occurrence of stray fragments of the typical black pottery at a number of them. Just why the immigrants should have chosen to settle at Baħrija is something of a mystery, since there is no convenient harbour nearby. Surprisingly enough, though, the inhabitants of the Baħrija settlement seem to have been richer than their neighbours in one way—they could afford to acquire more metal objects (at least to judge by the number of small fragments of metal which they lost or threw away). Finds of spindle-whorls, loom-weights and clay anchors were also far more numerous than at other sites, which might suggest that Baħrija was a centre for the industrial production of textiles for export. Perhaps the immigrant group from Italy was in some way specially connected with this trade.

The preference of the later Bronze Age inhabitants of Malta for settlements on inaccessible hilltops or defended by massive walls would seem to imply an unsettled state of affairs which lasted for several centuries. This emphasis on defence could reflect the danger of pirate raids, so often an important factor in Mediterranean life, or it could reflect an internal political situation in which each group, with its fortified settlement, was independent of, and potentially hostile to, every other. There may be some truth in both these explanations, but we shall probably never be able to find a definitive solution. In contrast to the ubiquitous fortifications, there has been a complete absence of finds of weapons, but since these would have been of bronze, they were no doubt melted down when they ceased to be of use.

PHOENICIAN AND PUNIC PERIODS

Though the earliest material of Phoenician type which has been found in Malta dates from the 8C B.C., no written documents which bear on the islands' history are available until much later. For another few centuries they were still virtually in a prehistoric stage. The early Phoenician material comes from rock-cut tombs, which continued to be the norm for burial right through the Punic and into the Roman period. A great mass of material has been found in the large number of such tombs which have come to light. The earliest are circular in plan, with a circular pit entrance. Later first the pit, then the chamber itself come to be square or rectangular in form.

Just how and why the Phoenicians first came to the Maltese islands we do not know. Probably they found the harbours useful as refuges from storms and pirates on their trading voyages to the W. The name Malta itself may come from the Phoenician *malat*, a port or refuge, but we do not know for certain that the Phoenicians called it by this name. They certainly called Gozo *gol*, which means a broad-beamed merchant ship, and there is some evidence that their name for Malta may have been *'onan*, a large ship. Perhaps they thought of the islands as a fleet of ships of different sizes! It seems possible that the flourishing textile industry of late prehistoric times may also have had something to do with their interest, however. Centuries later, in Roman times, the manufacture of fine textiles was still one of the staples of the islands' prosperity.

Some of these early Phoenicians did settle and were buried on the islands, but it is difficult to say just what their status was, or how far they were in control. They must have been in contact with the native inhabitants, but there is remarkably little evidence available bearing on this question. Many years ago a settlement site was investigated at Qallilija, near Mdina, which produced Late Bronze Age and Phoenician material, and stray objects of Phoenician type have been found on other Bronze Age sites, but this does not take us very far.

Another problem of this shadowy period is what relations the early Greek traders and colonists had with the Maltese islands at this time, if any. A certain number of Proto-Corinthian, Corinthian and Black Figure vases have been found in Malta, but these do not necessarily imply anything more than occasional trading, presumably with the Greek colonies of Sicily. The idea that there was a Greek colonization of the islands during the 7 or 6C B.C. rests almost entirely on a mistaken dating of Greek inscriptions and Maltese coins which really belong to the time when the islands had come under Roman domination.

Whatever the uncertainties as to the history of the Maltese islands during the 8 and 7C B.C., it is certain that in the course of the 6C B.C. they passed into the hands of Carthage, originally a Phoenician colony, which was at that time building up a trading empire in the West Mediterranean. For the first time in their history but by no means the last, the islands became of strategic importance. The Carthaginians were in process of consolidating their power in Sicily and the Gulf of Syrte, so that possession of the small, centrally placed island group became of vital importance to them in connection with their efforts to withstand Greek advance in this area.

For more than three centuries after this the Maltese islands remained a part of the Punic Empire. It seems very likely that the Carthaginians actually sent colonists to settle the islands, though we have no certain knowledge about this. The archaeological evidence is of no help in assessing the size of such a colony, since all the equipment used in this period seems to have been of Punic type, with, in the later part of the period, a growing number of imported Greek objects. However, it is noticeable that the islands seem to have been allowed a greater degree of freedom than most Punic satellites. For instance, they seem to have been allowed to trade freely with foreigners, which was most unusual. The Greek imports, and conversely the early popularity of the Maltese dog in the Greek world, are good evidence for this. Towards the end of the Punic period the Maltese seem to have even been allowed to strike their own coins, if scholars are correct in dating the first issues before the Roman occupation.

As already mentioned, most of the archaeological evidence for the Punic period comes from the rock-tombs. The objects which accompany the burials are mostly dull and repetitious, with occasional exceptions, which are usually imported Greek or Egyptian objects. One tomb yielded a fine clay sarcophagus which is a quite early example of a well-known Punic type which is based on the Egyptian mummy-case. The lid of this example is moulded into the shape of a female figure.

It has long been known from documentary evidence and from inscriptions in the Phoenician language found in Malta and Gozo, that the Carthaginians established important temples to their gods in both islands. There was known to be one in Malta dedicated to Melkart (later identified with the Graeco-Roman Herakles or Hercules), and another to his consort Astarte (the Greek Hera, Roman Juno). In the last few years large scale excavations by the University of Rome at the hill of Tas Silġ, near Marsaxlokk, have revealed that this was the site of the latter. This Punic temple was found to have been constructed over the remains of a Copper Age sanctuary, among whose ruins was found one of the characteristic stone statues of a fat sexless deity. The Punic building was a well-built complex of halls and courts of rectangular plan, with a store for the bones of sacrificed animals and for a large number of potsherds bearing dedications to two goddesses, Astarte and Tanit. These provided positive identification of the building. There was a ramp leading from the temple on its hill down to the port on the coast not far away.

The temple of Melkart was probably in the near neighbourhood of the Astarte-Tanit temple, since as long ago as the 17th century a stone *cippus* (small column) with a votive inscription to Melkart was found in the vicinity. This object has a special importance because the inscription recording the dedication by two brothers, Abdosir and Osirxamar, was cut into the base of the column in both Phoenician and Greek, and this bilingual helped considerably in the first decipherment of the Phoenician language. It is now in the Louvre. Another Phoenician inscription refers to the restoration of various temples in Gozo by the people of that island.

About the settlements of this period we know very little, probably because their remains now lie under modern towns and villages. We know that in Malta there were important ones at Mdina, Marsaxlokk and Birgu, but there were obviously others also. In the village of Żurrieq, for example, there is a very remarkable survival which could be a relic of pre-Roman architecture. The main part is a tower about 24 ft high made of massive rectangular blocks carefully dressed and well fitted together. This structure is crowned by a deep overhanging cornice which gives the building something of an Egyptian effect. This tower is now incorporated in one of the houses of the village, and some remains of other walls of similar character show that it was originally part of a set of rooms grouped round a rectangular courtyard.

The development of Roman power and the growing rivalry between Rome and Carthage brought on a period of unrest and suffering for the inhabitants of the Maltese islands during the 3C B.C. In the year 257 B.C., during the First Punic War, Malta was invaded by a Roman army under the Consul C. Attilius Regulus, and was thoroughly devastated and plundered. The Romans may have intended to occupy the islands permanently at this time, but if so their defeat in Africa two years later put an end to the plan and the Cathaginians returned and continued to hold them until 218 B.C. In that year, at the beginning of the Second Punic War, a Roman force under Sempronius finally took possession of the islands, apparently without a struggle, and probably with the connivance of the inhabitants, who handed them over, along with the Punic garrison, to the Roman consul.

ROMAN PERIOD

The Romans incorporated the Maltese islands into the province of Sicily. The archaeological evidence shows clearly that while the Punic culture and speech of the local people was at first little affected by the new political situation, a Greek element appeared which was of considerable importance, as shown by the striking number of inscriptions in Greek. It was even thought desirable to put a Greek translation of the dedication on the *cippus* of Abdosir and Osirxamar, already mentioned above, which probably dates from the 2C B.C. This situation is easily understandable, since the influence of the important Greek cities of Sicily was bound to be strong in the new situation. However, the great majority of the population undoubtedly continued to speak their native Punic dialect, just as Maltese is spoken at the present day. Whether this Semitic speech survived up to the time of the Arab invasion in the 9C A.D. is not known, but it seems perfectly possible. Such a survival would certainly make the rapid adoption of another Semitic language at that time more easily understandable.

The burials in the rock-tombs give us the same picture of the persistence of Punic tradition, which was only gradually modified by the influence of Graeco-Roman civilization. Cremation as well as inhumation is found in the tombs of the earlier Roman period, and objects of Greek or Roman manufacture or design occur in them mixed with objects, especially pottery, of Punic type. The tombs were often used and re-used over a long period, the earlier burials being simply pushed to the back. Clay oil lamps, which were always left lighted when the tomb was sealed, illustrate this continuity very vividly, since types of very different dates are sometimes found in the same tomb.

As time went on more elaborate types of rock-tomb were sometimes made, which were in the nature of small cemeteries incorporating a number of separate burial places for one or two bodies. These may sometimes have been owned by families, but others were those of guilds. One at Rabat seems to have been the property of a guild of weavers, to judge by the carvings of weaving equipment in the central hall; others of masons, tinsmiths, etc. Many of the simpler of these hypogea consist only of two short corridors, or a single hall, the individual graves opening about half way up the walls. Some, however, are more elaborate, consisting of an irregular collection of rooms, often having a small hall with a semicircular apse as the nodal point. These are often equipped with stone benches and a stone table, perhaps intended for the sharing of a funeral meal. The more elaborate of these rock cemeteries seem to date from the 4 and 5C A.D., though some may be older. The largest and most elaborate are the St Paul's Catacombs at Rabat. These seem to be definitely of Christian origin, and a few others can be ascribed to Christian communities with a similar confidence. Most produced no evidence bearing on the religion of their users, but many of these also may have been Christian. A few were probably owned by Jewish communities. None of the Maltese catacombs compare in size with those of Rome; in detail, they are most closely similar to those of Sicily.

The temples founded during the Punic period long kept their importance, and indeed seem to have attained, during the earlier part of the Roman period, an even greater international fame than they had earlier. So much has long been known from the references by Cicero in his prosecution of the infamous Verres, who was propraetor of Sicily (including the Maltese islands) from 73-71 B.C., for abusing his position and organizing the systematic pillaging of his province. Cicero refers specifically to his depradations on the treasures of the famous temples of Proserpine, Apollo and Juno in Malta. This last would now seem to have been identified in the temple uncovered by the Italian excavators at Tas Silġ. Here the Punic temple of Astarte-Tanit was extended on a lavish scale in Roman times. The new complex included a monumental portico and a fine mosaic pavement. Fragments of votive plaques of this period bear dedications to Hera (the Greek form of Juno, and also identified with Astarte). The temple of Juno seems to have recovered from Verres' spoliations, however, and continued to flourish for some time. During the 2C A.D. it seems finally to have been abandoned, and somewhere between the 4 and 6C A.D. a Christian monastery was erected on the site. The baptistery of this was situated right over the centre of the old temple, but other parts, including the church, have not yet been located.

The chief town in Malta during Roman times was on the site of the present day Mdina and part of Rabat. This had previously been the old Punic capital, so no change was involved. The large number of tombs and catacombs found in the area of Rabat confirm its importance. They lie just outside the area covered by the Roman town (which was somewhat larger than the present Mdina), in accordance with the Roman regulation forbidding burial of the dead in a town. Some vestiges of an important house of the Roman period have been uncovered, and a Museum has been built on the spot, which is misnamed the Roman Villa Museum (since the building in question was a town house, not a villa). Real villas have been identified and excavated at a number of places. They were well sited and commodious, and combine with all the other evidence about Roman Malta to indicate that the islands enjoyed a quiet prosperity during Republican and early Imperial times. Malta was famous during this time as a centre for the production of fine cloth, excellent sailcloth, and honey (the name Melita, if it does not come from the Phoenician *malat,* port or refuge, was probably derived from the Greek *meli,* honey).

The impression of prosperity and security is not seriously disturbed by the recent discovery that the massive 'round towers' whose ruins are found at various points around the coast, seem to have been erected in the Roman period. Few have yet been properly investigated, but it looks as though they were built near the beginning of Roman rule, when the Punic Wars were still raging and the islands were still an outpost of the developing empire. They could also have been used later during the period of the Civil Wars, or when piracy was rife, but one at least seems to have been converted into a farmhouse by the 1C A.D.

It is probably because it was a prosperous backwater in the centuries that followed the destruction of Carthage that we know so very little about the history of Malta during this period. Shortly after the assassination of Julius Caesar the Sicilians were given Roman citizenship, and presumably the Maltese with them. Otherwise documents are uninformative, and after the 4C A.D., there are no references until A.D. 533, when it is recorded that Belisarius, the general of the Emperor Justinian, called at Malta on his way to the reconquest of Africa from the Vandals. Later, during Justinian's war with Totila, the Byzantine general Artabanes took refuge there from a storm, and it seems clear that at that time the islands were firmly in the possession of the Eastern Roman Empire. The Byzantines once again made them part of the province of Sicily. It is during the Byzantine period that we first hear of a church hierarchy in Malta, though in fact it must have existed much earlier. The Byzantines remained in control until 870 when an Arab fleet appeared and took possession.

The most famous episode in Maltese history during the whole of the Roman period is undoubtedly the shipwreck of St Paul there in either A.D. 58 or 60 when on his way to Rome as a prisoner for trial. The circumstantial description of this event in Ch. XXVII of *Acts,* and of the subsequent welcome of the apostle by Publius, the chief man among the Maltese, whose father he cured of an illness, is vivid and convincing. Small wonder that the tradition is strong in Malta that Paul was able to lay the foundations of a Christian community there during his three month stay. Publius himself, so the story goes, became a bishop, first of Malta and later of Athens. The traditional location of the wreck of Paul's ship is St Paul's island, or Selmunett, on the N.W. side of St Paul's Bay. It has usually been assumed that the house of Publius in which he stayed was at Mdina, but the recent Italian excavations at the site of the 17C church of St Paul Milqi (St Paul Welcomed), which lies not far inland from St Paul's Bay, have revealed that not only was this the site of earlier churches, but also of a Roman villa, which by the 7C A.D. at latest had become a place of pilgrimage which was definitely connected with St Paul.

PREHISTORIC CHRONOLOGY

Period	Phase name*	Approx date
Għar Dalam Neolithic	Grey Skorba Red Skorba	5,000-3,750 BC
Copper Age	Zebbuġ Mġarr Ġgantija Saflieni Tarxien	3,750-2,200 BC
Bronze Age	Tarxien Cemetery Borġ in-Nadur Baħrija	2,000-1,450 BC 1,450-800 BC 900-800 BC

* adopted from 'type site'

MALTA IN LATER TIMES

Arabs and Normans. Malta's 'Dark Ages' are darker and longer than most, and the island barely emerges again into history before A.D. 870. Then it was conquered by the Abbasid Caliphs, already masters of the greater part of Spain, the s. part of France, Italy, and Sicily. Their influence lingers in the modifications they introduced into the kindred Maltese language, and in the introduction to the island of cotton and citrus fruits. Count Roger of Normandy, after delivering Sicily from the Arabs came in 1090 to the rescue of Malta. The national colours of red and white now embodied in the flag of Malta are supposed to stem from the blazon of the Hauteville family to which he belonged. A few Siculo-Norman palaces survive in Mdina.

The island shared the prosperity of the Sicilian kingdom under their Norman and Hohenstaufen rulers, with Christian and Moslem doubtless living in harmony as in Palermo. The death of Frederick II, the Angevin succession, and expulsion of the Moslems marked the second half of the 13C. After the Sicilian Vespers, Charles of Anjou attempted to use Malta as a base from which to recapture Sicily, but was defeated in a naval battle off Valletta. For the next century and a half Malta came under the Aragonese. The institution of the Università, a form of limited local self-government, was often vitiated by the practice of giving the island as a fief to some rapacious governor. In 1428 the Università redeemed the island in perpetuity from enfeoffment for a large ransom. The following year the islands were sacked by Barbary corsairs, not the first of many raids the frequency of which increased through the century. Until 1436 there seem to have been only two parishes, Mdina and Birgu, to which the other wayside churches were subordinate. In that year the ten principal settlements were raised to parish status.

The Knights of St John. By a deed of 24 March 1530, still preserved in Maltese archives, the Emp. Charles V made over Malta and its dependencies, in perpetual sovereignty, to the Order of St John of Jerusalem. The Grand Master's sole obligation was the annual presentation on All Saints' Day of a falcon to the Emperor's viceroy in Sicily. The Knights of St John, or Knights Hospitallers, had their origin in a small hospital and chapel inaugurated at Jerusalem for the use of poor and sick pilgrims to the Holy Sepulchre. The hospital, dedicated to St John the Baptist, was founded by merchants of Amalfi with the sanction of the caliph before relations between Christian and moslem had developed into a holy war. The order was thus primarily a nursing brotherhood. The first crusade ended in 1099 with the capture of Jerusalem by Godfrey de Bouillon. In 1113 Paschal II placed the Order and its possessions under papal protection. Its secondary preoccupation with the defence of pilgrims now inevitably became predominant and before long the white cross banner of the Order was spreading terror and dismay among the Saracen armies. Commanderies were formed all over Europe, stimulating zeal and regulating the finances of the Order.

The Knights shared in the great Christian defeat at Tiberias (in which their only English grand master was killed) and Jerusalem was lost to Saladin. In 1191 Richard Coeur de Lion established the Order in Acre, where they remained nearly a hundred years under twelve grand masters. When Acre was taken by the Sultan Khalil, they sought refuge in Cyprus in 1291. In 1310 Fulke de Villaret, after a struggle of four years, seized the island of Rhodes, and established the Order there.

In Rhodes the Knights built a powerful fleet and 'from being hospitallers first and soldiers second became sailors first and hospitallers second'. Pope Clement V assigned to them part of the property of the Templars who had been suppressed in 1312. For two centuries the Knights defied the Turks; they took part in the capture and later in the defence of Smyrna, and withstood two great sieges—in 1444 by the sultan of Egypt and in 1480 by Mehmet II. In June 1522 Suleiman I attacked Rhodes and laid siege to its citadel. Six months later the Knights capitulated on honourable terms. On 1 Jan 1523 Grand Master Villiers de L'Isle Adam, with 180 surviving brethen, left the island. They first retired to Crete and later to Malta.

The Order probably reached its developed form in Rhodes when it comprised three classes, the Knights of Justice, the Chaplains of Obedience, and the Serving Brothers. The military knights, who came to dominate the Order completely, had to prove noble birth without taint of illegitimacy for four generations on both sides of the family, and were thus the most exclusive aristocratic body in Europe. The conventual chaplains, not of necessity nobly born, served the hospital and conventual church. The brothers not only acted as servants but had military duties. For convenience in battle the order was divided into langues, or nationalities. These were eight in number; Auvergne, Provence, France, Aragon, Castile, England, Germany, and Italy. Each langue had its own Auberge, a headquarters building which was the military parallel to its legal equivalent the Inn of Court, with a pilier at its head. Its communal arrangements were not unlike those of a university college. At the head of the Order was a Supreme Council, consisting of the Bishop, the Prior of the conventual church, the Piliers of each langue, the priors, conventual bailiffs, and the Knights Grand Cross. It was presided over by the Grand Master, himself a Knight elected by his brethren.

L'Isle Adam arrived in the autumn and took possession of the fishing village of Birgu on Grand Harbour, leaving the Sicilian aristocracy aloof in Mdina. The fusion of the two traditions was gradual but that a tolerant relationship of all the elements in Malta was established within a generation seems proven by the unity of the defence against the Turks. The galleys of the Knights began to prey again on Moslem shipping and assisted in Philip II's sack of Peñon de la Gomera, a stronghold of the Barbary coast.

Many years passed before the Knights gave up hope of retaking Rhodes or moving elsewhere, an attitude reflected in the small scale of their early building operations in and around Birgu. Though all their military advisers advocated a new fortress on Mt Sceberras, this was not started. A source of revenue was lost when, in 1540, Henry VIII confiscated the forty-three commanderies and preceptories of the Langue of England. In Malta itself the Langue was still deemed to exist and the hope that counter-Reformation would revive it in reality survived for a century. Attacks on Malta and Gozo from the Barbary Coast became increasingly frequent in the 1550s.

In 1565 Suleiman the Magnificent, past his seventieth year, turned the whole strength of the Turkish dominions against his old enemy. The fleet was placed under Admiral Piali, the army under Mustapha Pasha, the two being designated co-commanders of the expedition. One hundred and eighty one ships sailed from the Golden Horn bearing upwards of 30,000 fighting men. The great Corsair Dragut (or Torgud) was to join forces with them. The defenders numbered between 600 and 700 members of the Order with a total force of 8000-9000 men. The Turkish landing was effected unopposed at Marsaxlokk.

Apart from a few cavalry skirmishes the whole campaign quickly resolved itself into the siege and defence of the fortified positions round Grand Harbour. The Turks concentrated first on reducing Fort St Elmo (comp. p. 82), then turned their attention to Senglea and Birgu, the two peninsulas either side of the Port of the Galleys. With a chain across the mouth and a bridge of boats across the water within, this formed one defensible stronghold. Throughout the long summer months all attacks were repulsed until at length the long-awaited and almost-despaired-of relief force from the Sicilian viceroy came to the island's release.

Valletta, founded immediately, quickly gained ascendency over Mdina and the renamed Vittoriosa, a position on which the seal was set when the Bishop of Malta transferred the curia from Mdina in 1622. A serious Turkish attempt to land in 1614 was driven off. The strategy and much of the spending of the 17C was based on the idea of a renewed Turkish threat. Throughout the century forts and look-out towers were built at strategic points on the coast. About 1720 these were supplemented by redoubts and batteries, many of which were later incorporated into the British defence system and so survive to this day. In fact, however, the Turks never recovered at sea from their defeat at Lepanto (1571) and after their route before Vienna were effectively contained in the Levant and the Balkans by larger European fleets and armies, By the end of the 17C, indeed, the Turks had trading agreements with Christian powers who soon protested against the Order's 'piracies'.

If as a European force the Order slowly declined through obsolescence into anachronism, as the sovereign power in Malta it transformed the island from a poor military base into a flourishing civil state. As military activities declined into privateering, the Order turned more attention to trade. After years of building fortifications and churches Maltese architects turned their hand to warehouses. Malta became a busy centre of entrepôt and transit trade when it was made a relatively cheap port in which to undergo quarantine. It also had a flourishing slave market. The population increased steadily and over the years grouped itself in a decreasing number of larger villages within reach of Grand Harbour. The cotton industry was encouraged to a point where exports of cloth became significant, but economically Malta subsisted on the revenues of its foreign estates and the incomes of the Knights themselves. They, less and less monastic in outlook, made their existence comfortable and even luxurious, a tendency which brought about periodic conflicts with the inquisitor, the bishop, or reforming grand masters.

The Knights' last serious participation in a military expedition against the Porte came in 1715-18 when they assisted the Venetians in their unsuccessful venture off the Peloponnese. The influence of the Knights on diplomacy and even on military decisions was over. As the political power of the Pope, their protector, diminished also, the strategic worth of Malta was increasingly canvassed in various chancelleries. The Order's possessions in France were confiscated during the Revolution, leaving them in financial straits.

On 9 June 1798 Napoleon, convoying 54,000 troops to Egypt, demanded permission to water his ships. When, as expected, this was refused, the islands were taken over with little resistance and the capitulation of Valletta followed. The impregnable fortifications were never put to the test. The Knights were given three days to leave, bearing only their holy relics and personal possessions.

The Order departed never to return and it was left to the Maltese to revolt against the new invader. Not content with looting the treasure of the Knights, the French despoiled the local churches and introduced various anti-clerical measures. A spontaneous uprising in Mdina was sparked off by the French commander's activities after the heartening news had reached Malta of Nelson's victory at the Battle of the Nile. General Vaubois withdrew his garrison of 4000 men behind the defences of Grand Harbour. The Maltese formed a National Assembly and sought British assistance. Nelson placed Capt. Alexander Ball in command of a blockading squadron. Later Ball took civil and military command of the insurgents and was reinforced first by Portuguese marines and later by 1500 British troops under Maj-Gen. Pigot. By the time the French had been starved into surrender in the late summer of 1800, the British were de facto rulers of Malta.

Crown Colony. Proposals to restore the Knights of Malta, under Russian or Neapolitan protection, met with vigorous Maltese opposition. They preferred what they had seen of British protection. British possession of the islands was confirmed by the Treaty of Paris in 1814, by which time the permanent importance of Malta as a naval base was established. As the century advanced the acquisition of more colonies in the E., the operations of the Crimean War, and the opening of the Suez Canal, all increased Britain's dependence on sea power based in the central Mediterranean. Development of commercial facilities was boosted by the opening of the Canal and for a time Grand Harbour shared with Aden the rôle of chief coaling station on the route from Britain to India and the Far East.

Representation of the Maltese people in the affairs of the colony was envisaged from the start and the first constitution was promulgated in 1835. New constitutions were introduced in 1849, 1887, and 1903, and in 1921 Malta was granted full self-government in all matters of local concern. The system did not work any better than earlier attempts and the constitution, suspended in 1930 and restored in 1932, was again suspended in 1933. Apart from the natural difficulties of an island group which cannot be self-supporting, other perennial problems were the official language controversy (for a long time it was Italian), and the economic difficulty of a civil administration geared to the vicissitudes of military expansion or contraction.

War once again united dissident voices and the second 'Great Siege' with its attendant ordeal by aerial bombardment began while the island was still unprepared. The epic stories of the three Gladiator fighters that in June 1940 took on the Italian air force for three weeks alone, and of the tanker Ohio towed in awash, with sufficient aircraft fuel to stave off inevitable surrender, reflect the more spectacular side of the privations suffered by the Maltese. Lack of food and of fuel, danger, dust, and long hours in underground shelters were the daily lot of everyone. But Malta's rôle was not entirely defensive. Her aircraft late in 1940 played an important part in Wavell's advance on Tripoli. Later her submarine and air attacks against enemy convoys to North Africa not only made supplying Rommel a costly affair but forced the Germans to reinforce Sicily with squadrons needed elsewhere. It was Rommel's successful advance that isolated Malta and made the first six months of 1942 the crucial testing time. The island was awarded its George Cross in April.

In proportion as Montgomery's advance from Alamein gathered momentum, the pressure on Malta lifted, and by the end of the year the invasion of Sicily was being planned from St Angelo and the Phoenicia Hotel. The political armistice between Italy and the Allies was signed aboard H.M.S. Nelson in Grand Harbour after secret military meetings in an olive-grove near Syracuse (Sept. 1943). On his way back from the Teheran conference Franklin D. Roosevelt visited the island and presented a Presidential Citation.

The British Government gave £30 million toward the reconstruction of war damage and in 1947 restored internal self-government. The idea of integrating Malta with the United Kingdom foundered on the problem of social security contribution as much as on religious difficulties. After a strained period when in 1959 the constitution was again suspended, Malta became independent in September 1964. Elizabeth II at the islanders' request assumed the additional style of Queen of Malta.

Under a Defence Agreement British Forces were entitled to remain in Malta for ten years. Under a Financial Agreement Britain undertook to provide, during the same period, capital aid in the form of grants and loans for the diversification of the economy and for assistance to emigration up to a total of £50 million.

The Malta Labour Party, under the leadership of Mr Dom Mintoff, won the General Elections held in June 1971. Soon after the elections the 1964 Agreements with Britain were renegotiated by the Maltese Socialist Government and a new Agreement, valid until 31 March 1979, was entered into which guaranteed a greater compensation to Malta for the use of military facilities by Britain for the defence purpose of the United Kingdom and of NATO.

Under the new Agreement Malta receives £14 million annually in rent and additionally received a sum amounting to around £7 million part grant and part soft loan and a further amount of £2.5 million in economic aid from Italy apart from technical aid from other countries.

By virtue of the Agreement the British Government and the other NATO countries accepted the principle that Malta was offering part of her territory for use for military purposes by foreign powers in order that, in the shortest possible time, she would be able completely to reconstruct her economy to enable her to do away with the need for any further economic dependence on a foreign military presence.

In Parliament on the 13 December 1974, several changes were made in the constitution of Malta and the country became a democratic republic within the Commonwealth. The office of President of Malta was established to replace the office of Governor-General and the monarchical system of Government under the Independence Constitution was abolished.

On the day Malta became a Republic the first Maltese born Governor-General, Sir Anthony Mamo, Q.C., B.A., LL.D., appointed by the present Socialist Government in July 1971, was nominated the first President of the Republic of Malta.

The Malta Labour Party was returned to power in the 1975 General Elections with 34 seats as against the Nationalist Party with 31 seats in a House of 65 seats.

Following the Labour Party's victory at the elections, the leader Mr Dom Mintoff was sworn in as Prime Minister, Minister of Commonwealth and Foreign Affairs and Minister of the Interior for another 5 year term on the 22 September 1976.

Sir Anthony Mamo was succeeded by Dr Anton Buttigieg, B.A., LL.D., as the new President of the Republic of Malta on 27 December 1976.

PRIME MINISTERS OF MALTA

1921-1923   Hon. Joseph Howard, O.B.E.
1923-1924   Hon. Francesco Buhagiar
1924-1927   Hon. Sir Ugo P. Mifsud, K.B.
1927-1932   Hon. Sir Gerald Strickland, G.C.M.G. (Lord Strickland)
1932-1933   Sir Ugo P. Mifsud, K.B.
1947-1950   Hon. Dr (later Sir) Paul Boffa, O.B.E.
1950 (Sept-Dec)   Hon. Dr Enrico Mizzi
1950-1955   Hon. Dr Giorgio Borg Olivier, LL.D.
1955-1958   Hon. Dom. Mintoff, M.A. (Oxon.)
1962-1971   Hon. Dr Giorgio Borg Olivier, LL.D.
1971-   Hon. Dom. Mintoff B.Sc., B.E.&A., M.A. (Oxon), A.&C.E.

PRESIDENTS

1974-1976   Sir Anthony Mamo
1976-   Dr Anton Buttigieg

REPRESENTATIVES OF THE CROWN AT MALTA
CIVIL COMMISSIONERS

1799-1801	Captain Alexander Ball, R.N., President of the Provisional Government
1801	Major-General Henry Pigot, in charge of the troops and of the Government
1801-1802	Sir Charles Cameron
1802-1809	Rear-Admiral Sir Alexander Ball, Bart.
1810-1813	Lieutenant-General Sir Hildebrand Oakes.

GOVERNORS

1813-1824	Lieutenant-General The Hon. Sir Thomas Maitland
1824-1826	General the Marquess of Hastings
1827-1836	Major General the Hon. Sir Frederic Ponsomby
1836-1843	Lieutenant-General Sir Henry Bouverie
1843-1847	Lieutenant-General Sir Patrick Stuart
1847-1851	The Right Hon. Richard More O'Ferrall
1851-1858	Major General Sir William Reid
1858-1864	Lieutenant-General Sir John Gaspard le Marchant
1864-1867	Lieutenant-General Sir Henry Storks
1867-1872	General Sir Patrick Grant
1872-1878	General Sir Charles Van Straubenzee
1878-1884	General Sir Arthur Borton
1884-1888	General Sir Lintern Simmonds
1888-1890	Lieutenant-General Sir Henry Torrens
1890-1893	Lieutenant-General Sir Henry Smyth
1893-1899	General Sir Arthur Fremantle
1899-1903	Lieutenant-General Lord Grenfell
1903-1907	General Sir Mansfield Clarke, Bart.
1907-1909	Lieutenant-General Sir Henry Grant
1909-1915	General Sir Leslie Rundle
1915-1919	Field-Marshal Lord Methuen
1919-1924	Field-Marshal Viscount Plumer
1924-1927	General Sir Walter N. Congreve, V.C.
1927-1931	General Sir John du Cane
1931-1936	General Sir David Campbell
1936-1940	General Sir Charles Bonham-Carter
1940-1942	Lieutenant-General Sir William Dobbie
1942-1944	Field-Marshal Viscount Gort, V.C.
1944-1946	Lieutenant-General Sir Edmond Schrieber
1946-1949	Sir Francis (later Lord) Douglas
1949-1954	Sir Gerald Creasy
1954-1959	Major General Sir Robert Laycock
1959-1962	Admiral Sir Guy Grantham
1962-1964	Sir Maurice Dorman

GOVERNORS-GENERAL

1964-1971	Sir Maurice Dorman
1971-1974	Sir Anthony Mamo

Grand Masters of the Order of St John in Malta

DE L'ISLE ADAM
1530-34 (French)

DE LA CASSIERE
1572-82 (French)

DE REDIN
1657-60 (Spanish)

ZONDADARI
1720-22 (Italian)

DEL PONTE
1534-35 (Italian)

DE VERDALLE
1582-95 (French)

DE CHATTES GESSAN
1660 (French)

DE VILHENA
1722-36 (Portuguese)

DE ST JAILLE
1535-36 (French)

GARZES
1595-1601 (Spanish)

RAFAEL COTONER
1660-63 (Spanish)

DESPUIG
1736-41 (Spanish)

DE HOMEDES
1536-53 (Spanish)

ALOF DE WIGNACOURT
1601-22 (French)

NICOLAS COTONER
1663-80 (Spanish)

PINTO DE FONSECA
1741-73 (Portuguese)

DE LA SENGLE
1553-57 (French)

DE VASCONCELLOS
1622-23 (Portuguese)

CARAFA
1680-90 (Italian)

XIMENES DE TEXADA
1773-75 (Spanish)

DE LA VALLETTE
1557-68 (French)

DE PAULE
1623-36 (French)

ADRIEN DE WIGNACOURT
1690-97 (French)

DE ROHAN DE POLDUC
1775-97 (French)

DEL MONTE
1568-72 (Italian)

DE LASCARIS CASTELLAR
1636-57 (French)

PERELLOS Y ROCCAFUL
1697-1720 (Spanish)

VON HOMPESCH
1797-98 (German)

PRACTICAL INFORMATION

GEOGRAPHY AND CLIMATE

The Maltese Islands, which consist of Malta, Gozo, Comino and two other uninhabited islands are situated in the middle of the Mediterranean Sea. There are no mountains or rivers. The coastline is well indented with harbours, bays, creeks and rocky coves and there are a few sandy beaches. The islands are small and the shoreline 137 Km around Malta and 43 Km around Gozo. The population is 310,000. The capital is Valletta. The seaport is Grand Harbour, Valletta. The airport is Luqa (6 Km from Valletta).

Month	Sunshine hours	Rainfall ins. mm.	Max F.	Max C.	Temperature Min F.	Temperature Min C.	Mean Monthly Sea Temp. C.
Jan.	5.2	3.26—83.5	63	17.2	46	7.8	14.3
Feb.	5.1	2.17—55.6	64	17.8	47	8.3	13.8
Mar.	6.9	1.58—40.5	68	20.0	48	8.9	14.1
Apr.	8.5	0.87—22.3	72	22.2	51	10.6	15.3
May	10.2	0.41—10.5	78	25.6	56	13.3	17.6
June	11.7	0.08— 2.0	85	29.4	63	17.2	21.3
July	12.6	0.02— 0.5	92	33.3	69	20.6	24.4
Aug.	11.9	0.22— 5.6	91	32.8	70	21.1	26.1
Sept.	9.1	1.19—30.5	86	30.0	69	20.6	25.0
Oct.	7.1	3.25—83.3	82	27.8	63	17.2	22.5
Nov.	5.9	3.39—86.9	74	23.3	54	12.2	19.4
Dec.	5.1	3.81—97.7	67	19.4	49	9.4	16.4

The mean figures in the table above give a fair general picture of the pattern of the Maltese climate. They are monthly averages and are taken over a period of 50 years for sunshine, 90 years for temperature and 100 years for rainfall. April, May, early June and October are probably the best months for an active visit, July and August being too warm for comfort. January is the least pleasant month and may indeed be as cold as London but much brighter. The day to day sequences, especially in winter, can be nearly as variable as those suffered in the British Isles. In summer it is generally fine and warm with pleasant N.W. breezes and virtually no rain. Occasionally, however, crops are withered and tempers frayed by the *xlokk* or sirocco, which blows from the Sahara raising the humidity uncomfortably. In September storms may presage the warm but showery months of October and November. The long winter hours of sunshine are punctuated by depressions when their warmth is dissipated by strong winds: the *majjistral* from the N.W.; the *tramuntana* from the N.; or the *grigal* from the N.E. Though frost is virtually unknown, hailstones are not. Gales are sometimes severe. Rainfall, though averaging c. 20 in. per year, can vary widely between years of drought with only 10 in. and of flood with as much as 40 inches.

APPROACHES TO MALTA

By Air

The national carrier is Air Malta. They have regular flights from London (daily), Manchester (twice weekly), Amsterdam, Brussels, Cairo, Frankfurt, Paris, Rome, Tripoli, Tunis, Vienna and Zurich arriving at Luqa Airport. Other schedule carriers include British Airways, Alitalia, UTA and Libyan Arab Airlines. Flights from London (Heathrow) take approximately 3 hours and both Air Malta and British Airways offer daily flights from November to March and frequency increases during April-October to twice daily flights or more during peak season of July-September.

Both airlines offer APEX fares which allow big savings on normal schedule fares provided they are paid for 21 days in advance and are for a minimum of fourteen days and a maximum of three months. Reductions can be more than 50% depending on time of travel.

For further information apply to Air Malta, St James House, 13 Kensington Square, London W8 (01-937 7181) or 24 Haymarket, London SW1 (01-839 5872) or to British Airways, 65-71 Regent Street, London SW1 or alternatively ring (01-370 5411).

By Land and Sea

For those travelling by car or rail, it is possible to make enquiries regarding cross channel ferries or rail communications through British Rail Passenger Enquiry Offices throughout Britain or by telephone (01-730 3440). Tirrenia Lines offer the following car ferry services from Italy to the island of Malta, once weekly from Naples (24 hours), three times weekly from Reggio di Calabria—Sicily, (15 hours). For further information on the Tirrenia Line Car Ferry Service contact Sealink Travel Ltd, 52 Grosvenor Gardens, London SW1 (01-730 3440 or 6357).

British drivers taking their own cars will find today many ferry companies operating crossings to the Continent and depending which they choose, there are multitudinous routes across France, Belgium, Luxembourg, Switzerland and Italy. Drivers need only take their vehicle registration book, a valid national driving licence (but should check if any of the countries they pass through require an International Driving Permit) and an International Insurance Certificate (the 'Green Card'). A nationality plate (eg GB) must be affixed to the rear of the vehicle so as to be illuminated by the tail lamp. The continental rule of the road is to drive on the right and overtake on the left. The provisions of the respective highway codes in the countries of transit, though similar, have important variations, especially with regard to priority, speed limits, and pedestrian crossings. Membership of the Automobile Association (Fanum House, Leicester Square, London WC2), the Royal Automobile Club (83 Pall Mall, SW1), or the Royal Scottish Automobile Club entitles motorists to many of the facilities of affiliated societies on the Continent and may save trouble and anxiety. The UK motoring organisations are represented at most of the sea and air ports, both at home and on the Continent, to assist their members with customs formalities.

The Sea Malta Company Limited, Europa Centre, P.O. Box 555, Floriana, Malta (Tel: 621262) has a ferry service linking Tripoli—Malta—Naples—Marseilles—Barcelona. For more information in the UK as to times of sailing and costs, contact—Aquitaine, Maritime Agencies Ltd., 2-4 York Rd., Felixstowe, East Anglia, Suffolk. Tel: (03942) 78888.

TYPES OF HOLIDAY AND ACCOMMODATION

Inclusive Holidays

Malta has become a very popular holiday venue and is packaged by some 60 tour operators throughout the UK. These operators use either scheduled airlines or charter flights, offering hotel accommodation and/or self catering accommodation and produce brochures showing the type of holidays they have available, with prices. Below is a short selection:

Cadogan Travel
159 Sloane Street
London SW1
Tel: 01-730 0720

Broads Travel
429 Birmingham Road
Sutton Coldfield
West Midlands Tel: 021 373 0228

Exchange Travel Agency Ltd.,
66/70 Parker Road
Hastings
East Sussex
Tel: 0424 434241

Fourwinds Holidays
8 Herbal Hill
London EC1
Tel: 01-278 8951

Maltatours UK Ltd.,
21 Sussex Street
London SW1Y 4RK
Tel: 01-821 7001

Maltavillas Ltd.,
40/43 Kenway Road
London SW5 0RB
Tel: 01-602 0221

Medallion Travel
182/184 Edgware Road
London W2
Tel: 01-724 1471

Silvair
Silvair House
13/14 King Road
Luton
Beds LU1 2DH
Tel: 0582 32612

Sovereign Holidays
P.O. Box 13
Victoria Terminal
Buckingham Palace Road
London SW1 9SR
Tel: 01-834 2323

Stanton Holidays
Pearl Assurance House
23 Princess Street
Manchester 2
Tel: 061 236 4872

Sightseeing Tours

Malta has many ground handling travel agents who offer the visitor sightseeing tours, and advice on the most suitable for their requirements can be obtained from the hotel. The travel agency booking offices are mainly Valletta and Sliema. They include:

Untours Ltd., Valletta   (Tel: 623640)
Touring Mediterraneo Ltd., Sliema   (Tel: 30618)
TWI Travelways International, Valletta   (Tel: 621756)
ABC Tours, Valletta   (Tel: 20431)
Alpine Travel, Valletta   (Tel: 627189)
Belair Travel Bureau, Sliema   (Tel: 36159)
Grand Tours Ltd., Paceville   (Tel: 36040)
A&V Brockdorff Ltd., Valletta   (Tel: 624312)
Thomas Cook Overseas Ltd., Valletta   (Tel: 625629)
Cassar & Cooper, Valletta   (Tel: 624226)
Cordina Steamship & Airline Co, Valletta   (Tel: 24702)
Euroholdings Malta Ltd., Sliema   (Tel: 39118)
Mifsud Bros, Valletta   (Tel: 28034)
Melitas Travel Agency, St Paul's Bay   (Tel: 73079)
Sullivan & Sullivan Ltd., Valletta   (Tel: 625946)
Sullivan Shipping Agencies Ltd., Valletta   (Tel: 22372)
Malta Holiday Services Ltd., Sliema   (Tel: 38104)
The Malta Steamship Co., Valletta   (Tel: 626123)
Malta Tourist Service, Valletta   (Tel: 626195)
Malta Tourist Transport, Valletta   (Tel: 24702)
Malta Tours Ltd., Paceville   (Tel: 38198)
Mondial Travel, Valletta   (Tel: 623900)
Olivair Travel Malta Ltd., Valletta   (Tel: 606857)
Panbert Travel, Valletta   (Tel: 27452)

The sort of tours available are:

1. A coach tour to the 'Cities of the Knights'—Cospicua, Senglea and Vittoriosa and a walking tour of Valletta
2. Mdina, Rabat and San Anton Gardens
3. The Tarxien Temples and the Hal-Saflieni Hypogeum followed by a trip to the fishing village of Marsaxlokk where the Turkish Armada landed and the Prehistoric Cave of Għar Dalam
4. A boat trip through the Blue Grotto and a coach trip to the Prehistoric Temples at Ħaġar Qim and Mnajdra
5. Malta Handicrafts village at Ta'Qali
6. Gozo. Coach and ferry to Victoria with a visit to Calypso's cave, Fungus Rock, Ġgantija Prehistoric Temples and Xlendi Bay.

Anyone interested in the seafaring history of Malta will want to take a cruise of the Grand Harbour and Marsamxett Harbour. These trips take place between 10.30 and 15.30 and leave from the quayside by Sliema and cost around £M1.25 for adults (children half-price). Other cruises leave here for the island of Comino at 9.00 hrs charging £M3.95 for the day's voyage, buffet lunch included, (children half-price). Companies organising such trips include Marsa Industries Ltd. Tel: 23754, Ripard Larvan & Ripard Ltd Tel: 31563 and Marsovin Ltd. Tel: 624918/6, Sunsea Cruises Ltd. Tel: 621217, 625066.

The Ministry of Culture offers a tour of specially selected sites once a fortnight on Sunday between October and May. Information is available from the National Museum, Republic St, Valletta. The price is around 50 cents and a picnic lunch should be taken.

Hotels

Malta has accommodation to suit a wide range of budgets and, according to the hotel or guest house category, official maximum prices are authorised by the hotels and catering establishment board. Many hotels offer substantial reduction during the off-peak period.

At the time of going to press the maximum tariff was as follows:

Hotel Category	Bed and Breakfast cents	Demi Pension cents	Full Pension cents
De Luxe	—	—	—
1A	650	800	925
1B	550	700	825
2A	480	620	730
2B	430	560	670
3	330	450	530
4	280	380	470
Guest House 1	280	—	—
Guest House 2	225	—	—

Listed below are the hotels in the De Luxe, 1A and 1B Category

MALTA AND GOZO

Category De Luxe

Corinthia Palace   (320 beds)
Attard, De Paul Ave, St Anton   (Tel: 40301)

Dragonara Hotel   (357 beds)
St Julians   (Tel: 36421)

Grand Hotel Excelsior   (376 beds)
Great Siege Road, Floriana   (Tel: 623661)

Grand Hotel Verdala   (328 beds)
Rabat   (Tel: 674901)

Malta Hilton   (400 beds)
St Julians   (Tel: 36201)

Hotel Phoenicia   (179 beds)
The Mall, Floriana   (Tel: 21211)

Hotel Ta'Cenc, Sannat, Gozo   (90 beds)
Tel: 76819

Category 1A

Cavalleri Hotel   (164 beds)
Spinola Road, St Julians   (Tel: 36255)

New Paradise Bay   (346 beds)
Paradise Bay   (Tel: 73981)

Preluna Hotel   (410 beds)
124 Tower Road, Sliema   (Tel: 34001)

Category 1B

Dolmen   (242 beds)
Qawra, St Paul's Bay   (Tel: 73661)

Fortina Hotel   (96 beds)
Tigne Sea Front, Sliema   (Tel: 30449)

Golden Sands Hotel   (226 beds)
Golden Bay, Ghajn, Tuffieha   (Tel: 73961)

Mellieha Bay Hotel   (428 beds)
Ghadira, Mellieha   (Tel: 73841)

Ramla Bay Hotel   (132 beds)
Marfa   (Tel: 73521)

Salina Bay Hotel   (200 beds)
Salina Bay   (Tel: 73781)

Tower Palace Hotel   (94 beds)
Tower Road, Sliema   (Tel: 37271)

INTERNAL TRAVEL IN MALTA

Roads

There is no longer a railway service in Malta so that leaves the main means of transport by road and water. There are three types of road— main asphalt roads linking major towns and villages. These are signposted, though not very well. The secondary roads between villages are asphalted but often only the width of a donkey and cart. They are interesting for those who like exploring, and they are very poorly signposted. However, if you drive in the direction of the place where you wish to go and do not deviate at alternative forks and crossings, you will usually arrive at your destination without too much trouble. Finally, there are country lanes which are unsurfaced and which will often peter out and leave you to retrace your steps.

Malta has gone metric and the speed-limit in built-up areas is now 40 km. per hour.

Maps

None of the maps are up-to-date owing to the road building programmes. The useful ones are the Malta Survey Map Ordnance Survey (scale 1:25,000), which comes in three large sheets, Malta East, Malta West, Gozo and Comino and the smaller Survey Map with a red front cover which is more manageable (scale 1:32,000). There is also The Maltese Islands Geographica 'Colourmaster' (scale:1:45,000) and an A to Z street map.

Buses

Buses run from the roundabout by the main entrance to Valletta—the City Gate Terminus—to all parts of the island of Malta, and from Victoria, the capital of Gozo to most villages on that island. It is usual to buy a ticket at the appropriate kiosk if you are boarding at a main terminal, passengers from intermediate points pay the conductor. Fares are very cheap (between 2½-9c) and tickets are inspected frequently. The buses on Malta are coloured light green and on Gozo light grey with a red band. For buses from Valletta see p. 63.

Self Drive Cars

There are car-hire firms in all the main towns and resorts and many leading hotels have car-hire desks in the lobby. Car-hire firms represented in London include Avis Rent-A-Car, (International Reservations), Station Road, Hayes, Midx; Hertz Rent-A-Car, (UK & International Reservations), 4-44 The Broadway, London, SW19; Godfrey Davis (Car Hire) Ltd, Davies House, Wilton Road, London SW1. Car rental in Malta is the cheapest in Europe and charges are Government controlled, at around £M3—£M4 per day, including insurance. The price also includes unlimited mileage and delivery to hotel or airport as required. It is advisable to take out full insurance because although the rule of the road is to drive on the left, it is common for local drivers to overtake on either side and for slow drivers to hog the outside lane.

A British or International driver's licence is required. There are many local car hire firms in Malta, should you decide to rent. The best place for advice is your hotel reception desk. If they cannot find a car for you locally, they should be able to obtain one from another town.

Karrozzin

The Maltese horse drawn victoria—the Karrozzin—was introduced in 1856 and is still used for sightseeing purposes. The fare is about £M1 to £M1.25 per hour and it is advisable to negotiate the cost before the start. Horse cabs can be found outside the Malta Hilton at St Julians, by the City Gate at Valletta, at Great Siege Square in Valletta and at the Customs House; in Sliema on the Promenade and in Mdina by Bastion Square.

Taxis

Taxis are very cheap and are identified by red number plates, with white numbers preceded by the word 'Taxi' also in white. Taxis are all fitted with meters and should charge Government controlled prices.

Approximate Taxi Fares from Luqa Airport To:

Valletta	75c
Mdina	£M1.10c
Marfa	£M2.00c
Golden Bay	£M1.75c
Sliema (Tower)	90c
St Julian's	£M1.00c

Malta-Gozo Ferry Service

A regular ferry service runs between Cirkewwa in Malta and Mgarr in Gozo all year round, weather permitting. Enquiries to Cirkewwa for weather 573430 and on Gozo Mgarr 76406. At the time of going to press new fares were under discussion. It is likely that the cost of taking a car across one way will be £M1 and a single passenger 10c. Motor vehicles should be at the quay 20 minutes before departure. The last bus leaves Valletta 75 minutes before the ferry's departure from Mgarr.

From 1 April to 31 May

Mondays to Saturdays		*Public Holidays and Sundays*	
Boat leaves Mgarr, Gozo	Cirkewwa, Malta	Boat leaves Mgarr, Gozo	Cirkewwa, Malta
06.15	07.30	06.45	07.45
09.00	09.45	09.00	09.45
13.15	14.15	13.30	14.15
15.30	16.15	15.30	16.15
17.30	18.15	17.30	18.15

From 1 June to 30 September

Mondays to Saturdays		*Public Holidays and Sundays*	
Boat leaves Mgarr, Gozo	Cirkewwa, Malta	Boat leaves Mgarr, Gozo	Cirkewwa, Malta
06.15	07.30	06.15	07.00
09.00	09.45	07.45	08.30
13.45	14.30	09.15	10.00
17.00	17.45	14.00	14.45
19.00	19.45	16.00	16.45
		17.30	18.15
		19.00	19.45

From 1 October to 31 March

Mondays to Saturdays		*Public Holidays and Sundays*	
Boat leaves	Cirkewwa,	Boat leaves	Cirkewwa,
Mgarr, Gozo	Malta	Mgarr, Gozo	Malta
06.45 (1)	07.30	07.00	07.45
09.00	09.45	09.00	09.45
13.45	14.30	14.00	14.45
16.00 (2)	16.35 (2)	16.00	16.35
16.30 (3)	17.15 (3)		

(1)   On Mondays, or, when a Monday is a public holiday, on the next immediately following day not being a public holiday, this trip will be performed at 06.15.

(2)   This trip is not performed on Fridays.

(3)   This trip is performed on Fridays only.

Water Taxi

The dgħajsa (pronounced 'dicer') is a characteristic harbour boat, with a high painted prow and is rowed in traditional fashion, standing. These water taxis can be hired from Customs House, Valletta or the waterfronts of Senglea and Vittoriosa. Charges are negotiable.

RESTAURANTS, FOOD AND WINE

When the last edition of the Blue Guide was produced the number of restaurants was limited. This was because there was little or no tourist trade and the Maltese preferred to eat at home. Since then the situation has changed considerably. Now, local specialities are to be enjoyed in a wide range of restaurants and some of these tasty dishes include:

Soup—*Minestra:* A thick vegetable soup, akin to minestrone. Another type of Minestra is made with beans and pork (Kawlata).

Pasta—*Timpana:* A case of flaky pastry, filled with a mixture of Rikotta cheese, minced meat, tomato puree, aubergines, onions and eggs and baked to a golden brown.

Fish—*Torta tal-Lampuka:* The Lampuka is a tasty Mediterranean fish. Slices of fish are fried and covered with pastry and then baked together with tomatoes, cauliflower, onions, olives and parsley.

Meat—*Bragioli:* Minced meat, bacon, eggs, onions and breadcrumbs wrapped in thin slices of steak and then deep fried.

Dessert—*Prinjolata:* This is a delicious concoction composed of a pyramid of sponge fingers held together with a mixture of butter cream, and almonds and decorated with melted chocolate and cherries and eaten at Carnival time.

Cheese—*Gbejna:* This is the most popular local cheese made from goat's milk.

Fruit—From December to March Malta grows oranges. Other fruit available at various times of the year are grapes, strawberries, melons, mulberries, tangerines and pomegranates.

Wine—Maltese wines are inexpensive. Among the local names are: Lachryma Vitis, Marsovin Special Reserve, Verdala, La Valette and 8th September wine produced by the Dept. of Agriculture. The question of which is most palatable is a matter of personal choice. For those who like a potent wine, Gozo produces the best choice. The visitor can also buy French, Italian and German wines in almost all restaurants on the islands.

Beer—Malta has local beers. Popular brands include Hop Leaf and Cisk, both of which are very pleasant.

Bread and Water—The bread in Malta is particularly good. The water, though not to everyone's taste, is safe to drink.

Restaurants are classified by the Hotels and Catering Establishment Board in Grades I, II and III. Listed below are the restaurants in the first two Grades.

Grade I

The Arches	Mellieha	Luzzu	St Paul's Bay
BJ's & Alley Cat	St Julian's	Medina	Mdina
Bologna	Valletta	Palazzo Pescatore	St Paul's Bay
Gillieru	St Paul's Bay	Winston	Sliema

Grade II

Alexandra's	Valletta	Barrel & Basket	Rabat
L-Ambient	St Paul's Bay	Bognor Regis	St Paul's Bay

Buskett Roadhouse	Rabat	Gardens Club	St Julian's
Chains	St Julian's	Hilltop	Mellieha
China House	St Julian's	Ta'Kolina	Sliema
Coleiro's Tavern	Marsa	Nigret	Rabat
Cordina Cafe/		Ogygia Palace	Gozo
Restaurant	Valletta	Paul's Punch Bowl	St Julian's
Eclipse	Gozo	It-Taverna	St Julian's
Il-Bancinu	Sliema	Tunny Net	Mellieha
Il-Barbone	Sliema	Whisper Knight	
Il-Fortizza	Sliema	Club and	
Il-Fekruna	St Paul's Bay	Farmhouse	Mosta
		Wyndhams	Sliema

MUSEUMS AND MONUMENTS

MALTA:

Għar Dalam and Museum, Birżebbuga
Hal Saflieni Hypogeum, Paola
Inquisitor's Palace, Vittoriosa
National Museum of Archaeology, Valletta
National Museum of Fine Arts, Valletta
National Museum of Natural History, Mdina
Palace Armoury, Valletta
Roman Villa and Museum of Roman Antiquities, Rabat
St Paul's Catacombs, Rabat
Tarxien Temples, Tarxien

Hours of Opening

From 1 October to 15 June

8.30 a.m. to 1.00 p.m.
2.00 p.m. to 4.30 p.m.

From 16 June to 30 September.

Monday, Wednesday and Friday:

8.30 a.m. to 1.30 p.m.
2.00 p.m. to 5.00 p.m.

Tuesday, Thursday, Saturday
and Sunday: 8.30 a.m. to 1.30 p.m.

GOZO:

Ġgantija Temples, Xagħra
Gozo Museum, The Citadel, Victoria

From 1 October to 15 June

8.30 a.m. to 1.00 p.m.
2.00 p.m. to 4.30 p.m.

From 16 June to 30 September

8.30 a.m. to 1.30 p.m.

Museums and Monuments in Malta and Gozo are closed on Public Holidays.

Visitors will not be admitted later than a quarter of an hour before the closing times specified above.

Admission Fees

	Persons over 18 yrs.	Persons under 18 yrs.
National Museum of Archaeology; National Museum of Fine Arts; National Museum of Natural History; and Palace Armoury	10c	5c
All other Museums and Monuments	5c	2c5
Comprehensive Day Tickets	20c	10c

No admission fees are charged at Ħaġar Qim and Mnajdra Temples, Qrendi-Ta' Ħaġrat Temples, Mġarr—Roman Thermae, Għajn Tuffieħa.

OTHER MUSEUMS AND MONUMENTS

Manoel Theatre, 81, Old Mint Street, Valletta.

Monday—Friday:	10.00 a.m. to 12 noon
	3.00 p.m. to 4.30 p.m.

Closed on Public Holidays
Entrance fee: Adults 5c.   Children 2c5.

St John's Co-Cathedral Museum and Oratory, Valletta.

Entrance fee: 25c (Covering entrance to the Mdina Cathedral Museum).
Entrance fee (Oratory only): 5c.

Monday—Saturday:	9.00 a.m. to 1.00 p.m.
	3.00 p.m. to 5.30 p.m.
Public Holidays:	9.00 a.m. to 1.00 p.m.

First Sunday of the month (other Sundays closed):-

Entrance Free.	9.00 a.m. to 1.00 p.m.

NOTE: Caravaggio's masterpiece "The Beheading of St. John" hangs in the Oratory.

Mdina Cathedral Museum.

Entrance fee 15c
Entrance fee 25c (covering entrance to the St John's Co-Cathedral Museum and Oratory)

From 1 October to 31 May.

Monday—Saturday:	9.30 a.m. to 1.00 p.m.
	2.00 p.m. to 5.00 p.m.

From 1 June to 30 September.

Monday—Saturday:	9.30 a.m. to 1.00 p.m.
	2.00 p.m. to 5.30 p.m.

Closed on Public Holidays.
First Sunday of the month (other Sundays closed):-
Entrance free.   9.30 a.m. to 1.00 p.m.

SHOPPING AND SOUVENIRS

Shopping Hours

Shops are generally open between 09.00 hrs and 19.00 hrs with a two or three hour lunch break. Shops are closed on Sundays and feast days. However, one food shop is open in each village until 10.00 hrs. Prices are fixed on all items. The best souvenirs include:

Malta Weave: This cloth is hardwearing and beautiful and ideal for making up into, skirts, dresses, bedspreads, cushion covers, and table cloths. The best place to purchase these materials either made up or in lengths is at the factory in St Catherine's Street, Rabat.

Glassware: Mdina glass is rapidly earning a reputation for good workmanship and the colours in the finished product are usually very attractive. The main factory and shop is at Ta'Qali.

Calcite Onyx: This material is found in only a few parts of Malta and Gozo and is made up into attractive jewel boxes, book-ends and lampstands. The workshops are at Ta'Qali.

Jewellery: The fine workmanship in filigree using both gold and silver is to be seen in shops all over the island.

Lace: Malta is renowned for its delicate lace. It has been the traditional craft for generations of the women of Gozo, who work in their own homes. It is sold at very reasonable prices.

Wrought Iron: Like many of the countries in the Mediterranean the people here excel in the use of this material and many workshops thoughout the islands are happy to welcome visitors.

The Malta Crafts Centre whose primary aim is to revive old crafts and encourage new ones is situated opposite St John's Cathedral in Valletta and houses a permanent exhibition of traditional and contemporary souvenirs genuinely manufactured in the Maltese Islands.

A Crafts Village at Ta'Qali is situated close to the old capital of Mdina. The workshops at the Crafts Village provide an excellent opportunity for the visitor to see hand-made articles being manufactured.

FESTIVALS

The History of Carnival

Carnival in Malta is held in the second week-end in May.

Carnival is of very ancient origin—a festival to end the dark winter and welcome the spring—but Carnivals in Malta as we know them now, were first organised shortly after the Knights came to the Island in 1530. The first that really broke out into general jollification was probably the Carnival of 1560, when a massed Christian armada was harbour-bound in Malta before sailing against Tripoli. The Genoese Grand Admiral sent his men ashore while Grand Master La Valette sanctioned the wearing of masks in public, which no doubt helped to ease their inhibitions.

Carnival is traditionally opened by the dancing of the Parata, a sword dance commemorating the Maltese victory over the Turks in 1565. Companies of young men or children—all dressed in costume and armed with wooden swords—take sides in equal numbers to represent Turks and Christians and dance in two concentric rings. The dance is directed by a leader who, blowing a whistle, strikes his sword against that of each of the men in the inner ring.

The dancers used to perform the dance on the Palace Square and later in front of the houses of persons likely to pay them for their trouble. Meanwhile, a stone was hung down from the 'Castellania', or Palace of Justice, which now houses the offices of the Medical and Health Department, as a sign that justice had been suspended for the three days of Carnival.

By the middle of the 18C, Carnival in Valletta was in its heyday. From 1751 onwards a rival Carnival attraction took place in Floriana a few weeks before Carnival proper and it too involved a procession of masks and carriages. The Order encouraged the craze by staging extra carnivals called "Mad Carnivals" for special occasions—the birth of an heir to the throne of Portugal, the enthronement of the King of Naples, each provided a suitable excuse for frivolity and fireworks.

It was usual for the Grand Master's carriage to head the Carnival procession and it would be flanked by cavalry marching to the beat of drums. The State Carriage was followed first by coaches and then by the processional carts.

The first half of the 19C was a poor time for carnivals. For one thing, the Knights had gone and with them their love of pageantry, for another, thousands had died during outbreaks of plague and cholera. These were years of misery and poverty. Nevertheless, some show of Carnival continued.

For many years now Carnival has been re-established as a season of general jollification. However, it is perhaps a mild comment on our times, that really spontaneous disorganized carnival fun is something rare except amongst young children. But you will find these small girls and boys, Queens in bedspreads and Turks in tablecloths, down many a side street in the city.

Holy Week Celebrations

In contrast with 'Merry Carnival', Holy Week is solemn and sombre.

On Maundy Thursday, after evening church service, people visit the 'Altar of Repose'; these altars are erected in all the churches, to commemorate the institution of the Blessed Sacrament by Jesus Christ. It is customary for the people to visit seven 'Altars of Repose' in their town or village, either on Thursday night or on Friday morning. Generally, the people pay their homage either in couples or in groups and it is a very moving sight to watch these small pilgrimages winding their way from church to church, reciting prayers all the time.

The Sacrament of the Holy Eucharist was instituted during the Last Supper. In Valletta, at St Dominic's Oratory, in Cospicua, at Pope Pius IX's Centre and at Lija, a traditional 'Last Supper' display is held which is open to the public on Wednesday, eve of Maundy Thursday and on Maundy Thursday. The 'table' prepared for thirteen (Christ and the twelve apostles) is laid with fresh leaves, wine-jars and pastries.

The climax of the Holy Week celebrations takes place with Good Friday pageants, when processions occur in some 14 towns and villages. Life size statues are carried by participants depicting episodes from the Old and New Testaments.

Easter Sunday is a day of rejoicing. The morning processions, with the statue of the 'Risen Christ' are held at Vittoriosa, Cospicua, Senglea and Qormi and these processions are in direct contrast with the solemn pageantry of Good Friday. This is the main out-door festivity celebrated on this day. The statue, accompanied by a brass band is carried by a group of young men at a very quick pace indeed.

Easter Sunday is a family feast for the Maltese. It is customary to visit one's relatives and even to exchange gifts. Of course, the Easter Egg is always present but the Maltese housewife prepares a special sweet for this day—"the figolla". According to mythology, the figolla used to be presented as a gift to Astarte—the goddess of fertility.

May Day

May Day (feast of St Joseph the Worker) celebrations are held in Valletta.

Mnarja

'Mnarja'—Malta's folk festival is held during the week-end preceding 29 June amid the greenery of Buskett Gardens, Rabat. This is an all-night traditional 'festa' with folk music and singing. Mnarja was so popular in the past, that the bridegroom had to promise his bride to take her to Buskett on Mnarja Day every year and the women used to put on their richest attire for the occasion. The word 'Mnarja' is derived from 'Luminarja' (illumination) because from time immemorial the countryside and bastions around Mdina used to be illuminated by torch lights and bonfires on the eve and on the feast itself. This event is brought to an end by horse and donkey races which take place during the afternoon near Mdina, Malta's medieval capital. It is a very spectacular race with the animals ridden bare-back.

Regatta

A Regatta in the Grand Harbour celebrates the failure of the Turks in 1565 and the Axis Powers in 1943 to cause Malta to surrender under siege. These festivities take place the week end around September 8th. The events include races between dgħajsas (oar propelled taxi-boats), whose gaily painted design is said to have originated around 800 B.C. in Phoenician times.

National Day

National Day is held on 13 December to commemorate Malta becoming a Republic. It is marked by parades, band music and fireworks in Valletta.

Festas

Every parish (64 in Malta and 14 in Gozo), has an annual day of festival determined by its patron saint not necessarily celebrated on that saint's day.

The celebrations begin with the triduum, a three days' service of prayer preceding the eve of the Feast. On the eve of the Feast Day, a Mass of thanksgiving is said in the morning. Bouquets of flowers are arranged around the imposing life-size figure of the Patron Saint in a central position in the nave of the church. On the day of the Feast brass bands play marches along the village streets and give a concert in the main village square, which is followed by a display of fireworks. In the evening the translation of the holy relic takes place. It is carried in procession from a side chapel to the High Altar. Solemn Vespers and Mass conclude the function.

Public Holidays

New Year's Day	1 Jan
Good Friday	movable
May Day	1 May
The Assumption- (Santa Marija)	15 Aug
National Day	13 Dec
Christmas Day	25 Dec

BANKS AND CURRENCY

Malta has a decimal currency with one Malta pound (£M1) being equal to 100 cents. Each cent is divided into 10 mils. And two pounds three cents and five mils is written as follows: £M2. 3c5. There are £M10, £M5 and £M1 notes and 50, 25, 10, 5 and 1 cent coins many of which bear a strong resemblance to the equivalent British pence coins. Also there are 5, 3 and 2 mils coins. Special silver and gold coins at values of £M50, £M20, £M10, £M5, £M2, and £M1 can also be obtained from the

Malta Coins Distribution Centre, Central Bank of Malta, Castille Place, Valletta. Permits to export these coins from Malta has to be acquired from the Central Bank.

There is no limit on the amount of foreign currency which may be brought into Malta but visitors are not allowed to take out more than £25M in local currency.

Hotels will cash travellers' cheques if backed by a bankers card and a passport. Better rates, however, are usually obtained from the banks and there are local branches in most towns. Banking hours are Monday to Friday between 8.30 and 12.30 and on Saturday 8.30 and 12.00. The law restricts the amount which can be changed on Saturday. Foreign exchange facilities exist 24 hours a day at Luqa Airport. The exchange rate at time of going to press is £M1 = £1.37.

The Bank of Valletta Ltd
Head Office
Republic Street
Valletta
Tel: 22431

Mid-Med Bank Ltd
Head Office
Republic Street
Valletta
Tel: 625281

Lombard Bank Malta Ltd
Republic Street
Valletta
Tel: 620632

Exchange Rates

The Central Bank of Malta issues the official Rates of Exchange for the Malta Pound. As these rates fluctuate, tourists are advised to enquire at the bank most of which have notice boards giving the up to date rate of exchange.

POSTAL AND OTHER SERVICES

The General Post Office is at the Auberge d'Italie, Merchants Street, Valletta. Other towns and most villages have offices and there are also sub-offices and agencies where stamps may be bought in Valletta and Sliema. Stamps can also be purchased in most hotels.

Letters and postcards to the United Kingdom go by airmail, daily. Airmail letters Malta to UK. First 15g costs 7c. Additional 15g costs 4c. Normal size postcards airmail cost 5c to all countries. Airmail letters from Malta to the rest of Europe 15g costs 7c. Airmail letters from Malta to the rest of the world, 15g costs from 11c to 20c, depending on destination. Overseas registration costs 10c plus postage. Express delivery fee on letters abroad is 10c extra. Internal letters 30g costs 2c. Local registration costs 6c plus postage.

Telegrams

Telemalta Corporation operates a 24 hour service from St George's Road, St Julian's (tel: 34042) for telegrams and telexes and from 7 a.m.-7 p.m. seven days a week at Luqa (tel: 25861). Telegrams only can also be sent between 7 a.m. and 7 p.m. Mon-Sat from St John's Square, Valletta (tel: 25719). Telegrams can be phoned to the above numbers.

Prices

Malta to Britain, Italy, France, and Germany. Telegrams (7 word minimum including address) costs 8c per word. Letter telegrams 4c per word with maximum of 22 words. Malta to USA and Australia. Telegrams (7 word minimum including address) costs 11c per word. Letter telegram 5c5 per word with maximum of 22 words.

Telephone

Local calls are on automatic dialling system and call box facilities are available. Telephone boxes are blue. Malta has telephone communications with most countries in the world and transferred charge calls are accepted in the UK. It is possible to dial direct to the UK, and to Italy. To other overseas countries, calls are booked by dialling 94 and 894 if you telephone from Gozo. To telephone London from Malta costs 60c per minute and it is also possible to book person-to-person calls (dial 94). To telephone the USA from Malta costs £M1.80 per minute.

For directory enquiries dial 90. Charges of up to 100% are usually made at hotels to callers telephoning overseas.

Useful Phone Numbers

Flight Enquiries	622901
Immigration Police	22941
Passport Office	25063
Customs	22921
Police Headquarters	24002
Posts and Telephones	24421
National Tourist Organisation	24444/28282/622915/22876
Prefix to call subscribers in Britain	044

CUSTOM HOUSE

Personal clothing and personal belongings, intended for the visitors own use, are not liable to duty if used. Each adult visitor is allowed free 200 cigarettes, or their equivalent in cigars or tobacco, together with 1 bottle of spirits and 1 bottle of wine and a reasonable quantity of perfumery/toilet waters not exceeding £M2 in value.

Duty Free Prices

Tourists visiting Malta are allowed to take back with them up to one litre of spirit or two litres of fortified wine, and two litres of table wine, one bottle of perfume and 200 cigarettes. A duty free shop is set up at Luqa Airport.

GENERAL HINTS

Electricity

240 volts/single phase/50 cycles

Health

The climate is generally healthy and under normal circumstances no inoculations are required by visitors coming from Europe, Australia, Canada and the USA. All hotels have the services of a local doctor available. There is a government hospital at St Luke's, Gwardamanġa (tel: 21251) and private hospitals, the Blue Sisters, Sliema (tel: 34063) and St Catherine of Siena's Hospital in Attard (tel: 42628). In Gozo there is Craig Hospital (tel: 76851). The health service in Malta has a reciprocal agreement for medical treatment with the UK providing for immediate medical care to British citizens. Tap water is safe but unpalatable.

Newspapers

Newspapers from the United Kingdom are available in Malta on the day of publication, in the morning or afternoon, depending on flight schedules from London. Continental newspapers may also be bought but their arrival in Malta is irregular.

Newspapers in English published in Malta are: "Times of Malta", "Malta News" and "The Bulletin" daily and the "Sunday Times of Malta", and "The Democrat", weekly.

Television and Radio

Xandir Malta, a division of Telemalta Corporation, provides broadcasting services under the overall supervision and control of the Broadcasting Authority. Television programmes include British and American productions. Besides live programmes broadcast by Television Malta, there is also good reception of transmissions from the two Italian television networks. In addition RTI (Radio Televisione Indipendente) operates a four hour daily programme service from Malta, at present on an experimental basis, for the Italian mainland. Radio Malta transmits daily on three services.

Time

Malta summer time (third Sunday in April until third Sunday in September) is two hours ahead of GMT. One hour ahead of GMT for the remaining months. For the correct time dial 95.

Youth Hostels

Headquarters at 17 Tal-Borg Street, Paola. Open 17.00 to 19.00 hrs weekdays. (Tel: 29361).
Residential Hostel 7 St Thomas's Street, Birzebbuga.

BEACHES

Sandy beaches are fairly limited on Malta. The best ones are to be found on the north and northwest part of the island. Most of them are suitable for non-swimmers and children except Għajn Tuffieħa and Ġnejna where at times warning notices signify when swimming is dangerous. There are plenty of sheltered coves and good rock bathing around St Julian's, Sliema and St Paul's Bay. Gozo has three sandy beaches—Marsalforn Bay, Ramla Bay and Xlendi Bay.

LANGUAGE

English is almost universally spoken. The only acquaintance the visitor need have with Maltese is sufficient ability to pronounce place-names. Maltese, a Semitic language supposedly Phoenician in origin, had been modified by later Arabic accretions before A.D. 1000. Many of the words added to the language in our millenium are of European origin, mainly from Italian or English, both of which languages have been widely understood and practised in the islands. Maltese is written in modified western characters. The alphabet has 29 letters: a b ċ d e f ġg għ hħ i j k l m n o p q r s t u v w x z ż. The vowel sounds are pure as in Italian, except that ie (as in Sliema) is a true diphthong. The following consonants have approximately the same pronunciation as in English: b d f k l m n p r t v. Ċ has the sound of ch as in church; ġ as English g in George (spelled Ġorg in Maltese); g as English g in go; għ is generally silent; ħ has a harder sound than h, but the two are not normally differentiable to an English ear; j as y in yet; q is virtually a glottal stop, comparable with the lack of sound accorded by a Cockney to the final t in that, or with the catch called the stǿd in Danish; s is always sibilant as in say; w as English w in wet; x as sh in shine; z has the sound of ts in cats or the German z in zehn, while ż is like English z in zebra.

The 24 Maltese consonants are divided into 'moon' letters (b f ġ g għ h ħ j k m p q v w) and 'sunny' letters (ċ d l n r s t x z z). Il, meaning the, retains its form before a moon letter, but modifies the l to the first letter of any noun beginning with a sunny letter. Ta' (of) becomes Tal (of the) by contraction and is equally subject to change, e.g.

Il-Knisja tal-Madonna ta' Fatima, Our Lady of Fatima Church but Iċ-Ċimiterju tad-Duluri, Our Lady of Sorrows Cemetery. Ħal (meaning village) modifies similarly.

Place Names

Since Malta achieved independence a 'pure' Maltese spelling has prevailed over the Italianate equivalents seen in most old maps. Place-names in this book follow the latest maps produced by the Directorate of Overseas Surveys, though variants are given where they are still widely in use. Names of streets are displayed bilingually in Malta and are given here in the English version as recorded in Baron Sceberras D'Amico Inguanez's admirable Street Guide.

BOOKS AND MAPS

The Maltese archives are extensive and much detailed work based on them has been published in Malta. The list here given is concerned in the main with more general works that are relatively obtainable in the United Kingdom.

Recent general introductions to the Maltese scene include *Luke, Sir Harry:* 'Malta' (2nd edn, 1960); *Bryans, Robin:* 'Malta and Gozo' (1966); *Hogg, Garı* 'Malta: blue-water island' (1967); *Brockman, Eric:* 'Last Bastion' (1961); *Kininmonth, Christopher:* 'The Brass Dolphins' (1957). *Ryan, F. W.:* 'Malta' (1910) is interesting for its account of bygone customs.

For Maltese prehistory the essentials are *Zammit, Sir Themistocles:* 'Prehistoric Malta: the Tarxien temple' (1930); *Evans, John D.:* 'Malta' (1959); and The Prehistoric Antiquities of the Maltese Islands (1971) and An Archaeological Guide (1971); and *Trump, D. H.:* 'Skorba' (1966); also the articles by the two last and *Bernabó Brea* in *Antiquity* vols. 34-37 (1960-63). These should all be read in the light of the introductory essay in the Blue Guide.

HISTORY. By far the best general survey is *Blouet, Brian:* 'The story of Malta' (1967), with a very well selected bibliography for further reading. The latest and most readable account of the Great Siege is *Bradford, Ernle:* 'The Great Siege; Malta 1565' (1961), based very largely on the eye-witness account of *Fr. Balbi di Correggio,* the original Spanish MS. of which is available in English in two translations both entitled 'The Siege of Malta', by *Bradford* (Folio Soc. 1965) and by *H. A. Balbi* (Copenhagen, 1961). For the history of the Order *Schermahorn, Elizabeth:* 'Malta of the Knights' (1929) may be supplemented by *Engel, Claire Eliane:* 'Knights of Malta: a gallery of portraits' (1963). Much further information may be found in *Cassar, P.:* 'A Medical History of Malta' (1965). *Hardman, William:* 'A History of Malta during the period of the French and British Occupations, 1798-1815' (1909) is a detailed study, but works on the later 19C in Malta are less easily consulted. They include *Laferla, A. V.:* 'British Malta' (Malta, 1947).

Of innumerable books on aspects of the Second World War may be mentioned: *'Bartimeus':* 'The Epic of Malta' (1943), propagandist but graphically illustrated by official photographs; *Lloyd, Sir Hugh:* 'Briefed to Attack' (1949); *Cunningham of Hyndhope, Viscount:* 'A Sailor's Odyssey' (1951); *Shankland, Peter and Hunter, A.:* 'Malta Convoy' (1961); *Gilchrist, R. T.:* 'Malta Strikes Back' (1945).

ART. *Hughes, J. Quentin:* 'The Building of Malta, 1530-1795' (1956) surveys the architecture of the Order in detail, but omits Gozo. There is no generally available equivalent for the Colonial period. *Sammut, Dr Edward:* 'Art in Malta' (Malta, 1954) is more important than its size would indicate, and the same author's short guides to 'The Co-Cathedral of St John' (1950); 'The Palace of the Grand Masters' (1951); and 'The Monuments of Mdina' (1960) are equally valuable.

In Malta the most comprehensive sources of ephemeral practical information are *Hilary, B. (ed.):* 'The Malta Year Book' (Malta, St Julian's, annually); 'Coming Events in Malta' (Malta Govt Tourist Office, weekly).

Maps. Essential to motorists and walkers alike are the excellent maps at 1: 25,000 (c. 2½ in. to the mile) published (1962-63) by the Directorate of Overseas Surveys. Malta occupies two sheets and Gozo (with Comino) one. These are readily available in London from Messrs Stanford's of Long Acre, W.C.2, or from bookshops in Malta. For detailed exploration of the villages the 'Malta Street Guide' (1958) by *Baron Sceberras D'Amico Inguanez* or A to Z of Malta and Gozo (1977) by J. G. Borg are invaluable.

EXPLANATIONS

TYPE. The main routes are described in large type. Smaller type is used for branch-routes and excursions, for historical and preliminary paragraphs, and (generally speaking) for descriptions of greater detail or minor importance.

ASTERISKS indicate points of special interest or excellence.

DISTANCES are given in kilometres cumulatively from the starting-point of the route or sub-route.—HEIGHTS are given in metres.

POPULATIONS are given to the nearest hundred according to the official estimates of 1977.

ABBREVIATIONS. In addition to generally accepted and self-explanatory abbreviations, the following occur in the Guide:

Adm.	admission
Bp.	bishop
C	century
c.	circa
Card.	cardinal
G.M.	grand master
l.	left
km.	kilometre(s)
Mons.	Monseigneur
r.	right
Rte	route
St	Saint
St.	street

Italo-Maltese Christian names:

Ant.	Antonio
Dom.	Domenico
Fil.	Filippo
Franc.	Francesco
Gerol.	Gerolamo
Giov.	Giovanni
Gius.	Giuseppe
Lor.	Lorenzo
Nic.	Nicolo
Stef.	Stefano
Vinc.	Vincenzo
Vitt.	Vittorio

MALTA

The **Maltese Islands,** are a group of five islands centrally situated in the Mediterranean. They are distant 93 kilometres from Cape Passero in Sicily and c. 290 kilometres from Cape Bon near Tunis, Gibraltar lies 1836 kilometres to the w. and Alexandria 1519 kilometres to the E. Between *Malta* itself, the principal island (246 sq kilometres), and its smaller sister, *Gozo* (67 sq kilometres), lies *Comino* (2.6 sq kilometres); the remaining islets, *Cominotto* and *Filfla,* are uninhabited. The total population of 308,940 is divided very unequally between Malta with 286,242 inhab. and Gozo with 22,700 of whom under thirty reside in Comino. The urban areas of the main island thus have a density of population hardly equalled in Europe. The capital, Valletta, on the N.E. coast of Malta, is situated in lat. 35° 53′ N.; long. 14° 32′ E.

Nowhere higher than 283 m, the island of Malta is geologically composed of sedimentary limestone with deposits of greensand and blue clay, and despite the proximity of seismic areas to the N. and W. is nowhere volcanic. The succession from the lowest stratum to the top is Lower Coralline limestone, Globigerina limestone, blue clay, greensand, and Upper Coralline limestone. In general the surface is flat, rising gradually towards the W. coast. The N.W., shattered by a series of faults, consists of bare limestone ridges and fertile depressions. There are no rivers and the rocky wieds are generally dry except during periods of heavy rain. With a low rainfall, there are few perennial springs and most domestic water is drawn from wells. About half of the surface is covered with a thin rich mould which proves surprisingly fertile since the island's small rainfall is restricted almost entirely to four winter months with long periods of drought in summer. Save for orchards of citrus fruits, carobs, figs, and olives, there are few trees. The principal danger is of soil erosion, especially during the frequent gales, and the island is everywhere criss-crossed with protective stone walls. These and the ubiquitous prickly pear leave an impression of barrenness, belied in April by the orange blossom and the crimson fields of silla, a clover grown for fodder. For the geology of Gozo and its consequences see p. 121.

The prosperity of the islands depended almost entirely for a century and a half on their importance to Britain as a naval and military base. In many obvious ways English influences have penetrated the Maltese way of life; they are not thought of as alien or to be shed with Independence. Indeed what has disappeared recently has rather been the faldetta, the traditional female headgear which was unique to the islands. Maltese schools have adopted British uniform styles almost exactly, so that in Valletta troops of children neatly dressed in blazers with pocket badges are rather more commonplace than they now are in London. The traffic keeps to the left; policemen wear helmets. Pillar-boxes and telephone kiosks are blue. Houses have suburban names, often untranslated into Maltese. The Maltese are a mixed Caucasian race stemming from the Phoenicians who colonised the islands during the 1st millennium B.C.

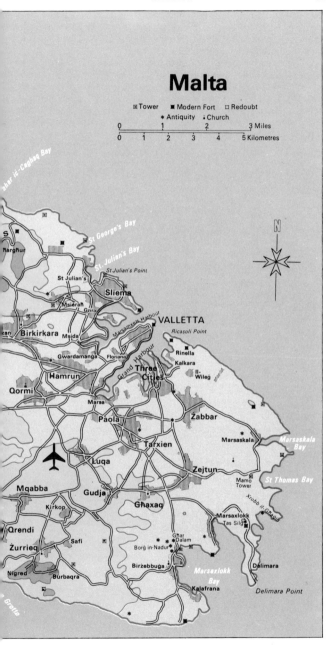

Malta

⊞ Tower ■ Modern Fort ▢ Redoubt
✳ Antiquity ⌁ Church

0   1   2   3 Miles
0   1   2   3   4   5 Kilometres

ħar iċ-Ċagħaq Bay

Baħar

St George's Bay

St Julian's Bay

Bargħur

St Julian's Point

St Julian's

Sliema

Msieraħ Gziri

VALLETTA

Birkirkara   Msida

Ricasoli Point

Gwardamanga   Floriana

Rinella

Kalkara

Hamrun

Three Cities

Il-Wileg

Qormi

Grand Harbour

Marsa

Paola

Zabbar

Tarxien

Marsaskala

Marsaskala Bay

Luqa

Zejtun

St Thomas Bay

Mqabba

Gudja

Mamo Tower

Kirkop

Għaxaq

Marsaxlokk

Tas Silġ

Xrobb il-Għaġin

Qrendi

Żurrieq

Safi

Għar Dalam

Borg in-Nadur

Delimara

Niġred

Burbaqra

Birżebbuġa

Marsaxlokk Bay

Grotto

Kalafrana

Delimara Point

With few exceptions they are Roman Catholic and the trappings of their religion are most typically Mediterranean. Like other Mediterranean peoples they use the street as the extension of their homes. They are devout, hardworking, cheerful, and intelligent.

The *casals*, as the villages are called, though seldom notable for great art, have the charm of an unfamiliar style of architecture with narrow streets designed as much to hinder an enemy as to further friendly progress. Their width served a donkey with panniers for many centuries before the coming of the motor-car. The dgħajsa, the characteristic harbour boat, with a high and painted prow is rowed in traditional fashion standing.

1   VALLETTA AND FLORIANA

A   The Centre of the city

VALLETTA, or *La Valletta,* the capital of Malta with 14,100 inhab., occupies the seaward half of Mt Sceberras (43 metres), the long rocky promontory which divides Grand Harbour from the harbour of Marsamxett. Founded by Grand Master La Vallette on 28 March 1566 on virgin rock, the city was designed by Franc. Laparelli and completed in 1571 by his assistant Gerolamo Cassar. Its plan comprises a rectangular grid of streets, twelve along and nine across the peninsula, with a perimeter road inside the fortifications. The streets follow the natural terrain with the result that many are steep or rise in steps, Byron's 'cursed streets of stairs'. Segregation of the knights into a Collachium, or inner citadel, was finally abandoned and the Auberges dispersed through the city to sites near the bastion to be defended by each Langue. The plan of the town has been little altered with the years and offers a unique example of a sea-girt fortified city of the Renaissance. Characteristic of the domestic buildings here, as elsewhere in the island, are the ubiquitous enclosed balconies, of painted wood, contrasting gaily with the golden stone.

Arrival by Sea. Landing from cruise ships in Grand Harbour is made at the New Quay, Marsa and at the Custom House, Lascaris Wharf (taxis), whence Liesse Hill leads directly into Valletta, or Crucifix Hill to Floriana.

Government Tourist Offices, Head Office, The Palace, Valletta. Tel: 24444; 28282. Information Office, 1 City Gate Arcade, Freedom Sq., Valletta. Tel: 27747.

Public Transport. Buses at the Valletta terminus (City Gate) link all the main villages and towns to the capital. The service is frequent and fares range between 2p and 9½p. Enquiries regarding times of departure can be made at the despatcher's kiosk or the police post at City Gate or by telephone 25916. Mini-Buses from here offer a perimeter tour of Valletta. The various destinations of the buses are indicated by route numbers and village buses stop at or near the parish church square. En route buses should be signalled to stop at a bus stop and the bell rung to alight.

Bus Route Numbers

Attard (St. Antons Gdns)	40	Marfa	45
Balzan	74	Marsa	1,2
Birkirkara	71	Marsaxlokk	
Birzebbugia (Għar Dalam)	11,12	(Fishing hamlet)	27
Cospicua	1,2	Mdina (Roman Villa)	80
Dingli (Buskett Gdns)	81	Mellieħa	44
Fgura	18,19	Mġarr	46
Għarghur	55	Mosta	53
Għaxaq	8	Mqabba (Hagar Qim)	35
Gudja	8	Msida	61
Gwardamangia	75	Naxxar	54
Gżira	60,61,62	Paola (Hypogeum)	5
Halfar	13	Pietà	61
Hamrun	71,73	Qormi	90
Kalafrana	12	Qrendi	35
Kalkara	4	Rabat (Catacombs)	80
Kirkop	34	Safi	33
Lija	40	St Andrews	68
Luqa Village	36	San Ġwann	65

Bus Routes (Cont'd)

Santa Venera	78	*Rocky Beaches*	
Senglea	3	Anchor Bay	44
Siġġiewi	89	Buġibba	49
Sliema Savoy	60	Għar Lapsi	89,94
Sliema Ferry		Marsaskala Bay	19
(Harbour Cruises)	61	Pwales Bay	43
Spinola	62	Qui-si-sana	62
Ta' Giorni	66	St Georges Bay	68
Tal-Qroqq	65	St Thomas Bay	26
Tarxien	8,11,15,26	Sliema Front	62
Ta' Xbiex	63A,64A	Slugs Bay	45
Vittoriosa Terminus	1	White Rocks	68
Vittoriosa Victory Sq.	2	White Tower Bay	50
Xgħajra	21		
Żabbar	18	*Sandy Beaches*	
Żebbug	88	Armier Bay	50
Żejtun	26	Għajn Tuffieħa Bay	47,52
Żurrieq (Airport)	32	Golden Bay	47,52
		Mellieħa Bay	44,48
		Pararadise Bay	45
		Pretty Bay	11
		Ramla Bay	45,48

History. A simple watch-tower seems to have stood on the tip of the peninsula when the Knights arrived. To guard the entrance to Grand Harbour Fort St Elmo was built in 1551. The first proposal to fortify Mt Sceberras was made by Antonio Ferramolino about this time, and Bartolomeo Genga died in Malta in 1559 after being called in as consultant architect. Another plan was drawn up in 1562 by Bald. Lanci of Urbino and the support of Pius IV obtained at the Council of Trent, but nothing had been started when the Turks occupied the peninsula as their base for the Great Siege of Birgu, the Knights' first capital. After the raising of the siege the Pope sent Laparelli to La Vallette; within three days of his arrival, he had prepared a new plan for a fortified city and the foundation stone of Valletta was laid on 28 March 1566.

The walled city of Valletta is separated from Floriana, its s.w. extension, by a terreplein, on which is laid out a vast piazza. In the centre plays the grandiose *Triton Fountain* by Vinc. Apap; to either side are the stands of City Gate Bus Station. To the w. the Phoenicia Hotel overlooks shady gardens. Protecting the city is a dry ditch, 17 metres deep and 9 metres wide, hewn from the solid rock by Turkish slaves, which extends for 875 m. between the two harbours. It is crossed by a bridge, from which (r.) we may see a lower bridge that in 1883-1931 carried a railway from Valletta to Mdina. *City Gate,* opening in St James's Curtain and protected by two bastions (see below), was tastelessly rebuilt in 1966. We pass under *Pope Pius V Street.* The open space to the right now *Freedom Square* was arcaded in 1968, is the site of the old railway station (comp. above).

Republic Street, the high street of Valletta, extends N.E. for 1½ kilometres along the spine of the promontory on which the city is built, terminating at Fort St Elmo. Named originally Strada San Giorgio, it was known during the French occupation as Rue de la République and subsequently as Strada Reale and then Kingsway and is closed to traffic except for shop deliveries in the early afternoon. It is thronged all day, but especially during the evening passeggiata. To the right are the melancholy ruins of the *Royal Opera House,* bombed in 1942. Designed by E. M. Barry, it was built (1861-64) on the site allocated to the Auberge of England and had already suffered once by fire in 1873. Beyond, to the right, is *St Barbara*, the church of the Langue of Provence, by Gius. Bonici (1739). The severe façade is adorned with a completely gilded figure of the Virgin. The church now serves English, French, and German catholics. The church of *St Francis*, on the left, rebuilt in 1681, has a celebrated roof painting by Gius. Cali, and is popular for evening devotions.

The **Auberge of Provence,** designed by Gerolamo Cassar in 1571, but subsequently considerably modified, has a symmetrical façade of two superimposed orders, Doric below, Ionic above. The central portico is given emphasis by the use of paired columns, set forward of the wall in contrast with the engaged pilasters of the wings. The building houses the **National Museum of Archaeology,** a collection based on the private accumulation of Giov. Franc. Abela, Maltese historian and student of antiquities, expanded and organized by Sir Themistocles Zammit in 1901-35.

Off the entrance hall we turn right for the PREHISTORIC GALLERY. Wall cases (r. to l.) display chronologically examples of the pottery styles from each phase of Maltese prehistory. *Case 1.* Impressed pottery from Għar Dalam, closely related to the Stentinello ware of Sicily. *Case 4.* Small contemporary stone model of a megalithic building, showing a simple plan and the method of roofing by slabs (c. 2000 B.C.). Later and more complete pottery from the temple sites and from tombs at Xemxija may be related to the models of the temples at Mġarr, Mnajdra, Haġar Qim, and Ġgantija (Gozo), and of the Hypogeum. On the left side of the gallery we may note bead necklaces, the incised Bull and Goat Plate from the Hypogeum, and a series of steatopygous idols from Haġar Qim. In a centre case the famous 'Sleeping Woman', a terracotta figurine from the Hypogeum, representing perhaps a patient or an initiate seeking in sleep an oracular dream (comp. the process of incubation used in Greece at Epidauros and elsewhere).

The TARXIEN ROOM contains further statuettes, including a more realistic skirted figure in terracotta on a straw core (perhaps a priest, rather than a goddess?), more sophisticated pottery, stone hammers and axes, and casts of the crude monumental sculptures from the temple at Tarxien. Tools are displayed of flint, an import from Sicily, and of obsidian, the most likely source of which was the Lipari Islands.

The Bronze Age came to Malta from the E. and the material in the BRONZE AGE ROOM bears no resemblance to and has no continuity with what went before. Objects from the Tarxien cremation cemetery include pottery, axes and daggers in bronze, together with ornaments and carbonized seeds (c. 1450-1350 B.C.). Pottery from the Iron Age village of Baħrija and from Borġ in-Nadur shows that a further wave of migrants arrived from the direction of Sicily and Calabria.

We return to the central lobby and turn right. The small room by the stairs contains various models of temples made in Neolithic times, whether as designer's or mason's working models, objects of piety, or charms is not known; triangular stone anchors; rollers on which the vast slabs were transported. Carved altars and blocks from the temples of Haġar Qim, Buġibba, and Xrobb-il Għaġin. The iron anchors on the top floor, raised from the sea bed, are from galleys of the Knights. The Roman and the Punic Rooms are being transferred in the near future to the top floor.

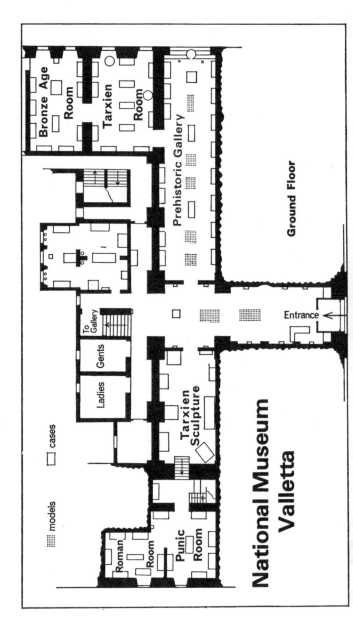

The TARXIEN SCULPTURE GALLERY is dominated by the mutilated lower half of a goddess statue originally c. 3 metres high. Opposite is a large block carved with a spiral decoration which may derive from Minoan-Mycenaean patterns. In the corner is a complete *Altar from the first apse of the s. temple group at Tarxien. In the stone cupboard in its face were found a flint knife and the horn of a goat.—The PUNIC AND ROMAN ROOMS, contain well-preserved articles (including Greek imports) from Punic rock tombs. Important are several Phoenician inscriptions, especially a votive cippus from the site of a Temple of Juno at Tas Silġ (Marsaxlokk) inscribed bilingually in Phoenician and Greek. Terracotta sarcophagus. Contents of tombs of Roman date showing local Punic ware in conjunction with a bowl made at Megara in Greece.

In St John's Square (r.) is the principal entrance to **St John's Co-Cathedral,** built in 1573-77 by G. Cassar, and until 1798 the conventual church of the Order. The entire expense of its erection was defrayed by Grand Master La Cassière and the church was consecrated on 20 Feb 1578. The building, which is remarkable alike for its historical associations, its architectural proportions, the richness of its decoration, and the wonderful diversity of its treasures, was embellished by successive Grand Masters and further enriched by the *gioja,* or present, which every knight was bound by statute to make on promotion. All but one of the Grand Masters are buried here, their tombs affording a veritable museum of Baroque sculpture. By a decree of Pius VII in 1816 the church was elevated to the status of co-Cathedral with St Peter and St Paul of the old city.

In plan the church is a plain rectangle. The severe FAÇADE, flanked by two bell towers, projects on the N. side a little beyond the width of the interior. The portico supports a balcony. The window above was enlarged to provide light for Preti's ceiling (comp. below). In the pediment is a bronze bust of the Saviour by Aless. Algardi; above, a 'Maltese' Cross, of eight points, the symbol of the Knights of St John of Jerusalem. The three faces of the clock, by Clerici, on the s. tower, mark the hour, the day of the month, and the day of the week. Over the door the arms of Pope Gregory XIII are flanked by those of the Order and of La Cassière.

The *Interior,* ornate but harmonious, consists of a single NAVE, 58 m. long with side chapels, the separating walls of which buttress the vault. Despite a width of 16 m. the apex of the slightly pointed tunnel-vault is only 20 m. above the floor. The horizontal line is further emphasized by the lack of entablature. This is replaced by an architrave which continues the pilaster capital mouldings across the intercolumniations. The ritual division of the nave from the choir is marked architecturally by a thickening of the vault rib and its supporting pilasters; as this is extended to the outside buttresses, it may be that a crossing and dome were projected From Corpus Christi to the Feast of St Peter and St Paul the nave walls are adorned with Flemish *Tapestries,* by Judocus de Vos (1697), based on paintings by Rubens and Poussin. The vault paintings (in oil directly on to primed stonework) were executed by Mattia Preti in 1662-67 at the expense of the Brothers Cotoner. They represent eighteen episodes in the life of St John the Baptist.

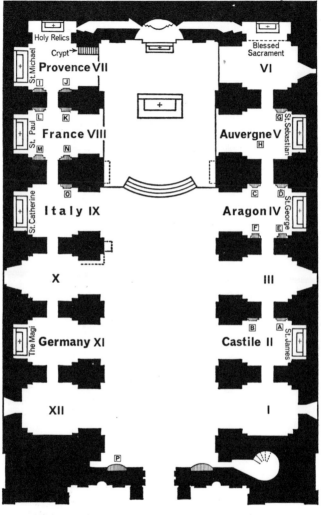

Co-Cathedral of St. John

Legend:

- A Vilhena
- B Pinto
- C Nic. Cotoner
- D De Redin
- E Perellos
- F Raf. Cotoner
- G De Chatte–Gessan
- H De Robles y Pereira
- I De Paule
- J Lascaris
- K J. de Wignacourt
- L Adrian de Wignacourt
- M De Rohan–Polduc
- N Louis–Charles d'Orleans
- O Carafa
- P Zondadari

The * *Pavement* is composed of some 400 sepulchral slabs laid in memory of the flower of the Order's chivalry. Constituted of marbles of every hue and adorned with coats-of-arms, heraldic emblazonments, military and naval trophies, instruments of music and war, mitres and croziers, figures of angels, crowns and palms of martyrs, skeletons and other symbols of death, the floor produces the gorgeous and striking effect of a stone carpet.

The SANCTUARY, raised on four steps, is closed by a marble balustrade. Within is the Archbishop's Cathedra. The two bronze *Lecterns* were presented by Francis of Lorraine in 1557 to the conventual church of Birgu. The *High Altar* (1686) is of lapis lazuli. Behind is a wooden *Lectern,* beautifully carved with scenes from the life of the Baptist. The gilded 16C *Choir Stalls* return against the E. wall. Above are a pair of organs. There is no E. window; in its stead the apse is filled with a colossal marble group of the Baptism of Christ, by Gius. Mazzuoli, 1644-1725, and a bronze *Gloria* by Giov. Giardini da Forti.

The **Chapels** were each allotted to a Langue of the Order. The small doors linking them were enlarged and arched by M. Preti to give almost the appearance of aisles. On the south side the first bay leads out to the Oratory of St John. The visitors entrance, is through the third bay. The second bay contains the CHAPEL OF CASTILE, LEÓN, AMD PORTUGAL (*St James*), decorated by Preti, contains the tombs of Manoel Pinto de Fonseca (G.M. 1741-73), and of Manoel de Vilhena (G.M. 1722-36), executed before his death by Massimiliano de Soldanis Benzis; the Grand Master is depicted on the relief panel examining the plan of Fort Manoel. The Byzantine ikon on the altar was brought to Malta in 1760 by the revolted Christian slaves of a Turkish man-of-war.

Turning right at the end of the third bay one can enter the Oratory of St John built in 1603 to provide a suitable place for knightly devotions and instructions to novices and decorated after 1662 by Preti. It has a fine 17C organ. Above the altar, is the Beheading of St John by Caravaggio the most important painting in Malta. Also on the altar is the monstrance made by Bernini for the reliquary containing the right hand of John the Baptist; the reliquary was looted by the French and went down in the 'Orient' in Aboukir Bay. The relic was given by Hompesch to Paul I of Russia. Stairs lead to the *Church Museum* where the tapestries, mentioned above, are normally kept. Also in the museum are a collection of beautiful embroidered vestments of the 17 and 18C as well as another painting by Caravaggio, St Jerome.

Caravaggio was made a Knight of Grace shortly after his arrival in Malta in 1607 but he was expelled from the Order after assaulting a Knight Justiciary.

The fourth bay is the CHAPEL OF ARAGON, Catalonia, and Navarre (*St George*), the altarpiece of St George was painted by Preti in Naples before 1657 and sent to Malta as a sample of his work. The other paintings, also by Preti, are later. A bronze medallion of Grand Master Ramón Despuig (1736-41) commemorates his decoration of the church. Two of the four Grand Masters' monuments should be noted: that of Nicolas Cotoner, ascribed to Dom. Guidi, and that of Ramón Perellos (1697-1702), by Gius. Mazzuoli of Volterra. Both artists were admirers of Bernini. The fifth bay is the CHAPEL OF AUVERGNE (*St Sebastian*) has two lunettes from the life of the saint, by Gius. d'Arena, though the altarpiece, also attributed to him, more resembles the work of Fil. Paladino. The monument is to Grand Master Clermont Gessan who reigned for less than a year in 1660. An epitaph in the floor marks the grave of Melchior de Robles y Pereira, who was killed in the siege.

The E. CHAPEL OF THE BLESSED SACRAMENT is closed by a screen and gates of silver (1752). Their colour is said to result from their being painted black in 1798 to escape the French. The Madonna di Carafa, bequeathed by Girol. Carafa, prior of Barletta, in 1617, was moved here in 1954 (Marian Year) from the chapel of Italy. It filled the gap left when the Madonna of Phileremos (originally brought from Rhodes) was removed by Grand Master Hompesch. The 15C crucifix, painted in tempera, also came from Rhodes. The keys on the walls, from Turkish fortresses at Mahometta (Hammamet, between Tunis and Sousse), Lepanto (Navpaktos in Greece), and Passava (near Gytheion in the Peloponnese), were captured by Admiral Gattinara in 1601.

In the seventh bay a door in the Sanctuary gives access, through the Chapel of Provence, to the CHAPEL OF THE HOLY RELICS, dedicated to St Charles Borromeo and allotted in 1784-98 to the Anglo-Bavarian Langue. The wooden figure of St John the Baptist on the left wall came from the poop of the Carrack in which the Knights sailed from Rhodes. From the *Chapel of Provence* (St Michael), we descend to the **Crypt,** which contains the tombs of all the first twelve Malta Grand Masters save Didier de Saint Jaille. The medieval style of their sarcophagi with full-length effigies is somewhat swamped by Nasini's exuberant decoration. Here, among others, are buried Villiers de l'Isle Adam, hero of the defence of Rhodes (tomb by Antonello Gagini, 1534); Jean Parisot de La Vallette who gave name to the city; Jean l'Eveque de la Cassière, founder of the church; Alof de Wignacourt (of the aqueduct); and the only person here below the rank of grand master, Sir Oliver Starkey, Turkopolier of England and secretary to La Vallette.

The eighth bay is the CHAPEL OF FRANCE (*St Paul*) which was stripped of its Baroque decoration c. 1840. It contains the tomb of Emmanuel Marie de Rohan-Polduc, last but one of the Grand Masters, who laid the foundation of the Maltese civil code. Also in this chapel are the earliest and latest monuments in the upper church: a simple marble urn of 1615 and the tomb of Louis Charles d'Orléans, count of Beaujolais, brother of King Louis-Philippe, who died in Malta in 1808; his full-length figure, by Jean-Jacques Pradier, was added in 1844. The ninth bay is the CHAPEL OF ITALY (*St Catherine*) which has as its altarpiece Preti's Mystic marriage of St Catherine. There used to be to the left of the altar, St Jerome, painted in Malta by Caravaggio (1608). But this has now been moved to the church museum for safe keeping. The bust of Grand Master Gregorio Carafa is by Algardi. In the tenth bay is located the north door of the cathedral which leads to Great Siege Square. The eleventh bay is the CHAPEL OF GERMANY, dedicated to the Magi. It was transferred to Germany from England only in 1631 (although the Langue of England was effectively suppressed by Henry VIII). The white marble altar is early 18C and the altarpiece is the Adoration of the Magi and the lunettes are by Stefano Erardi, late 17C.

In the last bay XII is the plain tomb slab of Mattia Preti (1613-99), who settled in Malta in 1661 and died here. He spent most of his time embellishing the island's churches, and his greatest memorial is the work he did in this cathedral. A further painting by him is to be found in the adjacent sacristy—Saints Cosmas and Damian. Other masterpieces include Antoine de Favray's portrait of Grand Master Pinto, and Perez d'Aleccio's painting of the Baptism of Christ.

We may leave St John's by the N. door, which opens into GREAT SIEGE SQUARE. A portico screens the N. wall of the cathedral. In the square an allegorical group by Sciortino commemorates the dead of the Great Siege of 1565. The *Law Courts,* opposite, replaced in 1967 the Auberge of Auvergne (an austere edifice of 1574 ruined by a bomb in 1942). A cinema in St Lucia's St. (l.) occupies the site of the house where Garibaldi stayed in 1864 (plaque).

Farther on we reach QUEEN'S SQUARE. To the left the Casino Maltese, the principal social club of the island, occupies the former Treasury of the Order. A marble statue of Queen Victoria (1897), by Giuseppe Valenti, stands before the arcaded façade of the **National Malta Library,** or *Biblioteca,* designed in 1786 by Stef. Ittar, a Calabrian architect, for the Order and completed in 1796. The collections now include 61,000 books, 50 incunabula, and 1250 MSS., as well as the records of the Università (or commune) from 1350 to 1818, and the priceless archives of the Order (6524 vols. of MSS.). The hours of admission vary slightly day by day, but the library is always open, Mon-Sat, 8.30-1.

In 1555 the Knights established a library where the books of their deceased brethren could be deposited, and passed a statute in 1612 forbidding the sale of a Knight's books at his death. The great bequests of Card. Giocchino Portocarrero (5670 vols) in 1760 and of Guerin de Tencin (9700 vols) in 1763 necessitated provision of a new building, which was decreed in 1776 and paid for by Perez de Sarrio. At the same time it was decided that the library should be opened to the public. The transfer of books may have been delayed by the French invasion for the building was not inaugurated until 1812.

The entrance steps are adorned with a bust of Dun Karm, who wrote the lyrics of Malta's National Anthem. A selection from the archives is permanently displayed. They include (despite some losses during the French occupation) documents from c. 1083 to 1798: deed of Baldwin I of Jerusalem (1107) giving land, the bull of Paschal II instituting the Order (1113), some of the records of the Templars before their suppression in 1312, letters from most European monarchs, the act of Donation of 1530 by the Emp. Charles V, minutes of councils from 1459, bulls of the chancellery from 1346, and the proofs of nobility submitted for admittance to the Order. A beautiful exhibit is the illuminated life of St Anthony the Abbot, by Master Robin Fournier of Avignon (1426).

Old Theatre St. descends (l.) to the Anglican cathedral (p. 77); between the library and the Palace (r.) and is where the busy street market popularly known as 'Fuq il-Monti' used to be, but this has now moved to St John's Square except on Sunday when it is held in St James' ditch.

Beyond extends PALACE SQUARE, where Dun Mikiel Xerri and 33 companions were shot by the French in 1798 for planning to open the city gates to the besieging islanders. The Palace fronts directly on to the street and the attention is drawn first to the Libyan Cultural Centre which faces it. This once accommodated the Grand Master's bodyguard and the Chancery of the Order. An inscription now covered up on the portico records the cession of Malta to Great Britain. Later the building was occupied by the Garrison Library and the palace quarterguard, which had its mess above. The building, which now houses the Italian Cultural Institute, is admirably set off by the flamboyant Hostel de Verdelin on the corner of Archbishop's Street.

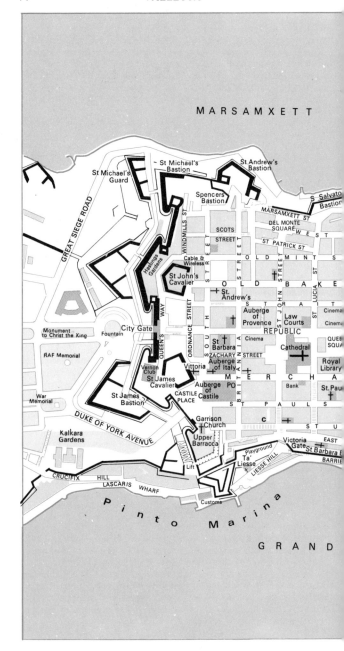

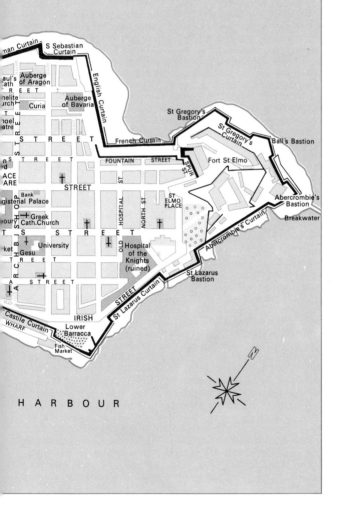

Valletta

| 0 | 100 | 200 | 300 | Yards |
| 0 | 100 | 200 | 300 | Metres |

HARBOUR

nan Curtain
S Sebastian Curtain

aul's
ath
Auberge of Aragon
R E E T
nelite
urch
Curia
T
noel
atre
Auberge of Bavaria

English Curtain

S T R E E T

French Curtain

St Gregory's Bastion

St Gregory's Curtain

Ball's Bastion

Fort St Elmo

FOUNTAIN STREET

STUR ST

Abercrombie's Bastion

Breakwater

Abercrombie's Curtain

STREET

ST ELMO PLACE

Bank
isterial Palace

Greek Cath.Church

oury

HOSPITAL ST

OLD HOSPITAL

NORTH ST

University

Gesu

Hospital of the Knights (ruined)

St Lazarus Bastion

STREET

St Lazarus Curtain

Castile Curtain
WHARF
IRISH
Lower Barracca
Fish Market

HARBOUR

N

The **Palace of the Grand Masters,** begun in 1571 by Gerolamo Cassar for Grand Master del Monte, incorporates the house erected for the master's nephew Eustachio two years earlier. This forms the N.W. corner of the palace and its balconies were matched for the sake of symmetry at the far end. The façade is 89 m. long and given coherence mainly by the roof line, unified in the late 17C, and by the balancing Baroque gateways which, in the time of G. M. Pinto (1741-73), replaced a single archway. The palace remained the official residence of the grand masters until 1798 and continued as that of successive governors and of the governor-general. Now it is the residence of the President of the Republic of Malta, and also the seat of the House of Representatives.

The right-hand gateway (or the entrance from Queen's Square) gives access to PRINCE ALFRED'S COURT, with a stately Norfolk Island pine. The clock, placed here by Pinto in 1745, has figures in Turkish costume to strike the hours. Below the two lions is an entrance to a modern staircase which leads to the great hall of knights 77 metres x 11½, which runs the full length of the palace above Merchants St. Part of this area is now given over to the House of Representatives. On entering the chamber the public gallery is placed in theatre style on the right and looks directly onto the floor of the House with the Labour Party's pews on the left, the Nationalist Party on the right and the Speaker's chair in the centre. By Prince Alfred's Court to the left is the entrance to the *Armoury (adm. see p. 49). By a statute of 1551 all arms and armour belonging to the Knights were pooled and kept in order at the public expense. The collection, though deficient in early armour and reduced by later neglect from c. 25,000 suits to under 6000 pieces, ranks in interest if not in richness, within the confines of its period, with those of the Armeria Real in Madrid and the Tower of London. It narrowly escaped removal to the Tower in 1827 and to Woolwich in 1846. Among many soldiers' suits are more resplendent ceremonial examples made for La Vallette and Wignacourt (Milanese, inlaid with gold); sapping armour of Wignacourt, of immense weight; fragments supposedly worn by Dragut during the siege; captured Turkish shields.

From King Alfred's Court steps descend to PRINCE OF WALES'S COURT, entered also from Republic Street by the left-hand gate. Here amid hibiscus and palm-trees stands a bronze *Statue of Neptune,* originally placed by Alof de Wignacourt as the centrepiece of a fountain in the old fishmarket in 1615; it has been conjectured to derive from a work by Giambologna, and to represent Andrea Doria. Behind under the arcade is a marble fountain with an elaborately carved escutcheon of Ramon Perellos. From the court a circular staircase, having shallow steps and wide anough to accommodate the grand master's litter, ascends to the STATE APARTMENTS (which may be viewed when not in use; apply to officials at head of stairs).

To the right the long *Armoury Corridor,* lined with portraits and armour, leads beteen the two courts; ahead extends the *Entrance Corridor,* similarly adorned and with a canvas ceiling painted by Nic. Nasini da Siena. In the lunettes above the windows are depicted naval battles of the Order. The three doors on the left of the Entrance Corridor lead into the *Hall of St Michael and St George,* formerly the Supreme Council chamber of the Knights. The frieze is painted with twelve incidents of the Great Siege, executed by Matteo da Lecce, a pupil of

Michelangelo better known from his work in Seville, as Mateo Pérez de Alisio. The hall acquired its present name in 1818 when the first investiture of the newly created British order was held here. At one end the throne used by the President stands on a dais; opposite is a sculptured wooden gallery with six cinquecento panels depicting scenes from Genesis. This was formerly in the palace chapel and may derive from a galley of the Order. The door to the left of the dais admits to the Red State Room, or *Hall of the Ambassadors,* the Grand Master's audience chamber. Below the coffered ceiling runs a frieze of scenes from the history of the Order between 1309 and 1524. The portraits include *Vanloo,* Louis XV; *Levitzky,* Catherine II of Russia; and *Lionello Spada,* Alof de Wignacourt, wearing the armour noted above (the painting was badly restored in 1886). The Yellow State Room, formerly the *Paggeria,* is the first room opening from the Prince of Wales Corridor. It contains a canvas of Jacob as a shepherd, by *Ribera.* The remaining rooms in this wing are occupied by the President and his staff (no adm.).

Off the Armoury Corridor is the Council Chamber of the Order, known as the *Tapestry Chamber* from the set of Gobelins tapestries presented by Perellos and signed by Le Blondel.

Beyond the staircase and overlooking Palace Square is the *State Dining Room.*—Coleridge occupied 'a suite of delightfully cosy and commanding rooms' during his residence in 1804-5 first as private Secretary to Sir Alexander Ball and later as Secretary to the Government of Malta. Some thirty years earlier Cagliostro was for a time G. M. Pinto's resident magician.

Republic Street beyond Palace Square becomes less interesting as it descends to Fort St Elmo (Rte 1C). The only important building is the *Borsa* (Exchange).

Archbishop's St. descends parallel to Old Theatre St. (comp. above) to Independence Square, crossing three of the streets that run parallel with Republic Street.

The first, STRAIT STREET (Strada Stretta), had a notorious reputation even in the days of the Knights, who disguised their duels there as casual quarrels occasioned by a collision in the narrow thoroughfare, since premeditated duelling was severely punished. In both World Wars it was known to servicemen as 'The Gut' and its more disreputable bars catered freely for a variety of tastes.

At the junction of Old Mint St and Archbishop Street is the *Curia,* or Archbishop's Palace, well restored in 1953. Facing Independence Square is the *Auberge of Aragon,* one of the plainest of the knightly headquarters, by Cassar; **St Paul's Anglican Cathedral** occupies the site of the Auberge of Germany, which was demolished in 1838 to make way for it. The church, to a design by Richard Lankersheer, was built by William Scamp at the expense of the dowager Queen Adelaide, widow of William IV, in 1839-41. Its prominent Gothic spire combines not unpleasingly with the classical style of the main edifice, their juxtaposition at ground level being hidden from view by clever siting. The organ was formerly in Chester cathedral. A plaque on St Paul's Building, beyond the apse, records Sir Walter Scott's brief stay at the former Beverley Hotel on this site in 1831.

Unobtrusive in Old Theatre St. is the **Manoel Theatre,** built in 1731 and claimed to be the oldest theatre in the Commonwealth, though 150 years junior in Europe to Vicenza's Teatro Olimpico. The interior was beautifully restored in 1960. Admission (from Old Mint St.) 10-12, also 3-4.30 in winter; 5c. The church of the *Carmine* is opposite. At No.

52 Old Bakery St. Dun Karm (comp. above) lived in 1910-36. The Bakery of the Order used to occupy the block, farther w., between St John's St. and Britannia St.

Returning to Palace Square and taking Archbishop's St. in the opposite direction, we pass the Greek Catholic Church and come to Merchants St., after Republic Street the most important thoroughfare in Valletta. The UNIVERSITY OF MALTA began here as a Jesuit college, instituted in 1592 by Pope Clement VIII, with faculties of philosophy and theology. In 1769, after the expulsion of the Jesuits from the island, Grand Master Emmanuel Pinto raised the college to university status, incorporating in it as a faculty of medicine the School of Anatomy founded by Nicholas Cotoner in 1674. A few years back the university moved to Tal-Qroqq. However the Jesuit buildings and the church of **Gesù** here remain substantially unaltered. If it was built in 1592-1600, it cannot have been designed (as is usually stated) by either of the Bonamici (Filippo or Francesco) since neither was yet born. In the left transept an inscription records the consecration here of Fabio Chigi (later Pope Alexander VII) as Inquisitor of the Order.

Above the high altar, Circumcision, attr. to *Bald. Peruzzi;* chapel of St Ignatius (r.), altarpiece by *Romanelli;* 3rd chapel (l.), *G. B. Caracciolo,* Flight into Egypt; 2nd chapel (l.), *Mattia Preti,* Altarpiece and two lunettes.

We pass between the rear façade of the Magisterial Palace and the animated covered *Market,* built in iron in 1859-62, where exotic fish and fruits provide a colourful display. Continuing up Merchant Street we come to the former *Banca Giuratale,* or Town Hall, an elegant building of c. 1720, now the Public Registry. Opposite is the *Monte di Pietà,* a government pawnbroking department, established on the continental model in the 16C and moved here by G. M. Ximenes. Behind this, in St Paul's St., the church of *St Paul Shipwrecked,* with an altarpiece of the shipwreck by Fil. Paladino.

On the next corner a plaque marks the site of the house of Sir Oliver Starkey. The main offices of Mid-Med Bank overlook the cloistered graveyard of the co-cathedral. At the corner of St John's St. is a column believed to have been a pillory or whipping-post. Beyond (l.), the Department of Public Health occupies the *Castellania* of the Order, begun in 1748 by Francesco Zerafa and completed by Gius. Bonici. Here the Castellano presided over the court of civil and criminal law. The pleasantly balanced façade has a centrepiece by Maestro Gian with figures of Justice and Truth.

The sober *Palazzo Parisio,* where Gen. Bonaparte lodged for a week in June 1798 on his way to Egypt, now houses the Ministry of Commonwealth and Foreign Affairs. Opposite is the *Auberge of Italy* which now houses the General Post Office. The building, begun by Gerol. Cassar in 1574, was improved and enlarged (probably by the addition of the top story) by Grand Master Carafa who, in 1683, placed his effigy and inscription above the rusticated portal. Once the headquarters of the Royal Engineers, it later housed the museum, and then the Law Courts, which have now been moved to their new building in Republic Street. Adjacent, but with its façade on Victory Square, is the church of the Langue of Italy, *St Catherine's,* designed by Gerol. Cassar in 1576, with a porch added in 1713, to the design of Romano Carapecchia. The interior, octagonal in plan, has an altarpiece of the

Martyrdom of St Catherine by Mattia Preti; notable also, Our Lady of Sorrows, by Benedetto Luti.

Facing is *Our Lady of Victory,* or La Vittoria, the first building to be erected in Valletta in thanksgiving for the Turkish defeat. The façade was added before 1690 when Ramon Perellos placed a bust of Innocent XI above the central window. Outside the church annually (Sun. after 16 Jan) pet animals are blessed. To the side is a statue of Paul Boffa, former Labour Prime Minister.

We turn left into Castile Place passing in front of the ***Auberge of Castile,** the grandest and most harmonious example of Maltese Baroque, reconstructed by Cachia for G. M. Pinto in 1744 and probably inspired by the Prefettura at Lecce. The portal is flanked by massive bronze cannons; above, the arms of Emmanuel Pinto are conspicuously displayed. The building is now the offices of the Prime Minister. Castile Place is bounded by the massive wall of *St James's Cavalier,* which now shelters the government printing press and the annexe houses the 'Annona' where handicrafts of Malta are on sale. From the E. corner of the square, to the left of the Mail Room of the GPO, open **Upper Barracca Gardens,** with a terrace affording a magnificent vantage-point over Grand Harbour. Originally an exercise-ground of the Langue of Italy, the space was given roofed arcades in 1661 but the roofs were subsequently removed. Among the statues in the gardens 'Les Gavroches', after the inspiration of Hugo's gamins, is considered the masterpiece of Sciortino, and there are monuments to Lord Strickland, Sir Winston Churchill and other heroes of the past.

In the corner a huge passenger lift used to descend to Lascaris Wharf.

Between St James's Cavalier and the Central Bank of Malta, Pope Pius V Street, crosses City Gate to St John's Cavalier, on the bastion of which are laid out the *Hastings Gardens.* The gardens, which contain a monument to the Marquess of Hastings, governor in 1824-26, are continued along the curtain to St Michael's Bastion and afford good views towards Mosta and Mdina.

Returning to the entrance to Valletta via South Street we come on our left to the Museum of Fine Arts. It is housed in a palace that was among the first to be erected in the city after the Order took up residence in 1571. The site was acquired in 1571 by Chev. Fra Jean de Soubiran. Later it became the property of the Order who leased it to various knights. The palace was rebuilt in its present form between 1761 and 1763. It passed through the hands of several famous personages and on 1st January 1821 was leased to the Naval Authorities and became the official residence of the Admiral Commander-in-Chief and was known as Admiralty House. It was presented to the Maltese Government in 1961 and officially opened on 7 May, 1974, as the **Museum of Fine Arts.** (Open 8.30-1 p.m, 2-4 p.m. Mon to Sun.)

The viewing galleries have been set out in chronological order. ROOMS 1 and 2 are 14C and 15C respectively with a fine Madonna and Child by *Domenico de Michelino.* ROOMS 3 and 6 are 16C and include paintings from Venetian and Dutch schools, with a Man in Armour by *Domenico Tintoretto* and a Portrait of a Lady thought at one time to be a *Holbein* and now believed to come from the circle of *Jan Van Scorel.* ROOMS 7 to 13 are 17C. Among this collection are some well displayed paintings by *Mattia Preti, Mathias Stromer* and *Guido Reni* as well as some unpleasant paintings by artists of second rank in the violent S. Italian style. The eleven rooms 14 to 24 contain art pieces from the 18C to 20C including works from *Antoine de Favray, Claude Joseph Vernet, Louis de Cros, Antonio Sciortino, Stafano Erardi, Edward Caruana Dingli, Francesco Zahra* and many contemporary artists.

In the basement there are a further five rooms, 25-30, showing relics of the Order and particularly fascinating is a model of one of the Knight's man-of-war 18C ships. The furniture on the ground floor is Maltese and Sicilian and pertains to the 17 and 18C.

B   Floriana

FLORIANA, a suburban extension of Valletta, was laid out to a plan of 1724 within the forward line of defences which began to be erected in the grand-mastership of de Paule and takes name from their architect.

In 1634 in face of a threatened new Turkish attack, Urban VIII sent Paolo Floriani to Grand Master de Paule to advise on additional defences. The Floriana lines were started in 1636, held up when the Margherita lines (Rte 4) were begun in 1638, but resumed in 1640 after a visit by Giovanni de' Medici. They were eventually completed by Grunenberg and de Tigné. The existing street plan dates from 1724-28 and many of the central blocks from before 1760.

Leaving Valletta by Castile Place we descend Duke of York Avenue. Below on the left *Kalkara Gardens* occupy a terrace above the Sir Paul Boffa Hospital and afford a fine view of Senglea and its creeks across Grand Harbour. To our right a deep ditch protects *St James' Counterguard.* At the bottom of the hill stands the *War Memorial.* Behind it (l.) is the Europa centre, headquarters of Air Malta.

Pleasant gardens extend N. to the Phoenicia Hotel (comp. Rte 1A). Prominent in their centre a golden eagle crowns the *R.A.F. Memorial* and in front of the hotel a *Monument to Christ the king,* by Ant. Sciortino, commemorates the International Eucharistic Conference of 1913.

To the W. extend THE MALL and the parallel Sarria St. Between them the *Maglio Gardens,* a tree-lined walk, was originally laid out by Grand-Master Lascaris as a ground for young knights to exercise at Pall-mall, in order to divert their thoughts from women, wine, and gambling. A statue of Vilhena that once adorned Fort Manoel, stands at the entrance and the monuments to various Maltese worthies include one to Sir Adrian Dingli unveiled by Edward VII during his second visit to Malta as king in 1907. On the right a huge *Parade Ground,* Independence Arena, which is now used as a sports ground. ST PUBLIUS SQUARE (l.), patterned by the circular slabs that cover its subterranean granaries, admirably sets off the façade of *St Publius,* the huge parish church of Floriana, erected in 1733-68. The design is attributed to Gius. Bonici but the façade is recent. The side chapels and their external screen walls were added in 1856. Beyond is the little church of *Sarria,* built on a circular plan by Mattia Preti in 1678. It is adorned with seven vigorous paintings by Preti. Opposite, at the end of the Mall, is a circular water-tower of the Wignacourt aqueduct (comp. Rte 9), which was built in order to supply Valletta with water from the hilly surrounds of Mdina. Part of the aqueduct is still in use. Nearby is an incongruous but not unpleasing Gothic of the Methodist church, which has now become a cultural centre. On a bastion (r.) the *Argotti Botanical Gardens,* administered by the university, contain a fine collection of cacti, exotic trees, and flora of the islands.

From the end of the Mall, St Chalcedonius St. leads past Police Headquarters and through the defences by Notre Dame Gate. By a steep descent under Salvatore Bastion, Sa Maison Rd., its continuation, passes below *Sa Maison Garden* (a nursery which supplies other public gardens) and through the outer defences to reach Pietà Creek (Rte 2).

We descend to join ST ANNE ST., the broad arcaded main street of Floriana. The road out has on one side the British High Commission and on the other the US Embassy, passes the *Porte des Bombes,* a ceremonial gate erected in 1697-1720 and now isolated from the walls. Looking back we see in a garden (r.) a striking bronze of Dante. We may return by *Gunlayer Square,* where gardens laid out along the bastions command the docks and anchorages of Grand Harbour.

C The Fortifications

The Fortifications of Valletta, to the design of Laparelli, were erected between 1566 and 1570 and are structurally largely unaltered. They are temporarily abandoned with the result that it is not usually possible to penetrate within the cavaliers and ravelins. Some of the walks and gardens on the bastions and along the curtains have been described above, but the best idea of the magnitude of the constructions is obtained by walking their circuit. The walk (c. 1½ hrs), affords in addition the varied panoramas of the two harbours and a convenient way of visiting Valletta's peripheral monuments.

From the Vilhena statue in the Mall, GREAT SIEGE ROAD descends between the Phoenicia Hotel and former Lintorn Barracks under the defences of Valletta. To the right rise the protecting walls surrounding St John's Bastion and St Michael's Counterguard. On our left and below, the Excelsior Hotel occupies St Roque's cove and commands excellent views of Marsamxett Harbour. On the left is Manoel Island with Ta' Xbiex farther left and Dragut Pt to the right. We reach the rocky shore and turn E. some 14 m. above the water.

On the right a road (restricted access) leads through the man-made canyon that constitutes the Great Ditch to Grand Harbour. Passing inland between St Michael's Counterguard and St Michael's Bastion, amid the rock-cut defences, it passes under City Gate bridge and Duke of York Avenue, and beyond the former Barracca lift joins Lascaris Wharf.

Great Siege Road now rounds *St Andrew's Bastion,* beyond which we curve over the lower Marsamxett Coast Road (with a popular bathing place) to pass within the curtain wall. Marsamxett St. fronts Mattia Preti Square which, with the two populous streets behind, is set at an angle to the grid plan of Valletta. Here a natural cleft was partly worked to form a '*Manderaggio'* (comp. the Mandraki of Rhodes), or sheltered harbour. For a time builders of houses had to take stone from this site, but the project was abandoned unfinished.

From Mattia Preti Square St John's St. mounts to the Cathedral.

Beyond *San Salvatore Bastion,* a popular belvedere, we pass below the conspicuous spire of the Anglican cathedral along the *German Curtain.* We turn the corner of St Sebastian St. and pass in front of the Carner Palace (1696), in which the Anglo-Bavarian Langue was installed during its short existence in 1783-98. The auberge stands above the inconspicuous *Jews' Sally Port,* which readmits to the city from Marsamxett Coast Road (comp. above). The *English Curtain* continues to an ancient sentry-box on the next corner whence the *French Curtain* extends to Fort St Elmo.

Fort St Elmo, the headquarters of the Malta Land Force (no adm.) occupies all the point commanding the entrances to both harbours.

Fort St Elmo had its origin in a watch tower which is first mentioned in 1481 and took name from a small chapel dedicated to the patron saint of sailors. A fort was erected in 1488 and strengthened in 1551 by Spanish military engineer Pedro Pardo. The main work was star-shaped with a protecting ravelin facing Marsamxett harbour and a cavalier on the sea front communicating with the main work by a wooden bridge. This was the fortress that in 1565 defied the whole might of the Turkish army for 31 days.

The Turks encamped on Mt Sceberras, placing their batteries on the Marsamxett flank where they were screened from the fire of St Angelo. This left open communication between Birgu and St Elmo of which the Knights at first made full use. Fourteen guns operating from a range of 165 m. kept up a continuous barrage. A sortie to destroy the battery was countered by a janissary attack which stormed the counter scarp. On 3 June the Turks captured the ravelin by surprise and but for a Spanish officer who held the drawbridge single-handed would have captured the fort itself. Here the Turks mounted two guns, soon reducing the ramparts of the fort to rubble. Dragut now constructed a battery on the point that still bears his name. Further assaults were repulsed. Dragut placed another battery on Ricasoli Pt and extended the lines in front of St Elmo to the water in order to cut the garrison's communication with Birgu. While directing these works. Dragut was mortally wounded. An assault on 22 June was again beaten off, a relief attempt from St Angelo was frustrated by the batteries, and on 23 June St Elmo fell. The operation had cost the Turks 8000 men.

Under Alof de Wignacourt the Vendome bastion was added, and in 1687 Grunenberg enclosed the entire point with a bastioned line, to which Grand Master Perellos added further works, so that it is difficult now to imagine the circumstances of the Great Siege. During the rebellion of the priests against G. M. Ximenes, the conspirators captured the fortress. The casemates that now serve as barracks were designed by Tigné in 1790. Captain Ball, first civil commissioner of the island, is buried in one bastion and Sir Ralph Abercromby in another. Both bastions and the Cavalier were again reconstructed to modern needs in 1871-75.

The road zigzags in front of the main entrance to St Elmo where more subterranean *Granaries* of the Order are marked by the familiar circular covering slabs. *St Lazarus Bastion* is built over, but its curtain, fronting the hospital, commands a good view of the entrance to Grand Harbour and the *St Elmo Breakwater* built in 1861 to protect it from N.E. gales and its warships from torpedo attack. The iron bridges that once spanned the small boat passage, just under the fort, were brought down by explosive motor-boats in a brave but abortive Italian attack on Grand Harbour on the night of 25 July 1941.

To commemorate the second siege of the last world war, when the Axis powers attempted to subdue Malta, a War Relics exhibition was inaugurated in 1975. This exhibition is the responsibility of the National Museum Association, a purely voluntary organisation formed to assist Government in setting up a War Museum. (open 8-1 pm, 2pm-4pm Mon-Fri [1 Oct-June 15]. 8-1 pm Mon-Fri [16 June-30 Sept]. 9.30-5.30 pm Saturday [All the year round]. 9.30-12.30 pm Sunday [All the year round]. Closed on Public Holidays. Adm. Free.)

During the siege there were 3,343 air raid alerts and 16,000 tons of bombs dropped. On 15 April, 1942—at the height of the Blitz—King George VI awarded the George Cross—the highest decoration for civilian gallantry—to Malta. At present the George Cross is on display at the National Library.

This Exhibition at Fort St Elmo, with its entrance at the end of the French Curtain, contains numerous interesting items. The main exhibit is the restored Gloster Gladiator 'Faith' which together with two other

Gladiators formed Malta's only aerial defence when Italy declared war on 10 June 1940. These three aircraft—which became famous for their heroic defence of the island were nicknamed "Faith, Hope and Charity". There is also the Jeep—"Husky", used by General Dwight D. Eisenhower before the invasion of Sicily in July 1943. Other interesting items are historical photographs of Malta in war-time and a captain's uniform donated by Earl Mountbatten of Burma.

The **Great Hospital of the Order,** or *Sacra Infirmeria,* is sadly only a shell after the bombing and shows an unbroken façade to the harbour. The hospital, was built before 1575 by an unknown architect. Restoration has begun to convert the building into a new conference centre and a new road is planned to facilitate access. Its plan seems to have been inspired by the Santo Spirito in Rome and the great ward, one of the longest rooms in Europe (155 m.) was well appointed if badly lit. In winter it was hung with 131 pieces of woollen tapestry; in summer adorned with 85 paintings by Mattia Preti. The second great court fronting on Merchants St. was added in the second half of the 17C.

The hospital was placed on the s.e. seafront of the town so 'that patients might be landed from ships at the mouth of the harbour, and brought in by a covered way below the sea wall into the lower ward, without making a tedious and dangerous circuit of the streets'. Its comparatively unhealthy site, sheltered from more bracing winds but open to the enervating sirocco, did not prevent it becoming the most famous institution of its kind in Europe. Patients, from outside the Order, ate from silver plate, and the hospital also cared for the insane and for destitute and illegitimate children. The French ejected its patients (and melted down the plate to pay for the Egyptian campaign). It was reopened as a British military hospital. In 1919 it became the headquarters of the Malta police.

Lower Barracca Gardens, occupying part of Castile Bastion above Mġerbeb Point, with a view across the entrance of Grand Harbour towards the Bighi Hospital, have an absurdly charming memorial to Sir Alexander Ball in the form of a Doric temple. *Castille Curtain* and *St Barbara Bastion* continue to a point in the walls below the Franciscan convent and church of *Ta Gesù,* where a natural cleft has resulted in an area of complex levels and steps. Here the *Victoria Gate* gives access by Liesse Hill to the **Marina.** The church of *Notre-Dame de Liesse,* on the descent, was rebuilt in 1740 at the expense of the Langue of France and is a graceful composition on a circular plan. Best seen from the walls above is the fine low dome moulded with bands of curved stone.

In the time of the Knights the old Del Monte now renamed Victoria Gate and Nixmangiari Steps served as access to the city. The new gate and road were constructed in 1884-87 and gave vehicular access to travellers arriving by sea. Since air transport this approach is seldom used except by cruise passengers, and regular bus services have all but killed the ferry approach from the Three Cities.

Barriera Wharf, where the fish market now stands, dates from before 1643 when it was used as a place of quarantine. Grand Master Lascaris turned the foreshore into a commercial wharf, building warehouses on both sides of the *Tunnel* by which he pierced the bastion bearing his name. On Lascaris Wharf stands the **Custom House*, the graceful masterpiece of Gius. Bonici (1774). Almost opposite is the Barracca Lift (no longer in use). To the s.w. Crucifix Hill ascends to Floriana.

Pinto Wharf continues along the shore below Floriana's defences to the main passenger ship berths. All along are warehouses inaugurated by various grand masters from Cotoner to Pinto.—From the top of Liesse Hill steps at the end of Battery St. ascend to the entrance of the Upper Barracca.

2   SLIEMA AND ST JULIAN'S

At the landward end of Floriana, beyond the Porte des Bombes, we diverge right (vehicles left, passing beneath the Hamrun road) and descend Princess Melita Road. On the left is the Protestant cemetery of Ta Braxia; on the right Jubilee Grove, a fine plantation, hides the glacis of Floriana's outer defences. At the foot of the hill, by a small children's park opened by Prince Philip in 1960, Sa Maison Road (p. 81) winds off into the defences. Marina St. follows the shore of Pietà and Msida Creeks, skirting Gwardamanġa Hill on the top of which, in the district called **Pietà** (*Sa Maison Hotel,* opp. Prince Philip Park) rises the unlovely bulk of St Luke's Hospital and medical school.

The Villa Gwardamanga is said to have been the residence of the Grand Master's taster. Occupied by Earl Mountbatten, it gave hospitality to Princess Elizabeth while the Duke of Edinburgh was on Malta station.

At the head of MSIDA CREEK the road divides at a roundabout. Msida and Birkirkara lie ahead. First right is the new regional road which leads out passing the University of Malta on the left and links up near St Julian's with the main coast road to St Paul's Bay and Mellieha Bay; further right is the direct road to Sliema via Gzira. Though longer it is more pleasant to keep to the shore of Msida Creek, past *St Joseph's,* the parish church of Msida, and take the less frequented road via **Ta'Xbiex.** All along the creek are yacht berths under the supervision of the Yachting Centre. Across the water the defences and the hotels of Floriana are prominent as we round another point into LAZZARETTO CREEK, once (as its name implies) the quarantine anchorage. It is now the principal *Yacht Basin* and always lined with sea-going pleasure cruisers. At the head of the creek, by pleasant gardens, we join an alternative road from Msida (comp. above). We are now in **Gzira,** which has developed largely since 1965 as a residential area with light motor industries.

A bridge on the right leads to **Manoel Island,** where FORT MANOEL, built by de Tigné and de Mondion in 1723-32 for Grand Master Manoel de Vilhena, was designed for a garrison of 500 men. Here in 1800 the French garrison was interned until (after the Treaty of Amiens) the men were returned to France in British ships. The island, previously called Bishop I., was first used as a quarantine station by the Knights, who erected an infectious disease hospital, the *Lazaretto of San Rocco,* before 1643. Though in ruins or in popular occupation, a great part of the lazaretto still stands, its graceful arcaded frontage on the sea forming a familiar landmark from the ramparts of Valletta.

Bad outbreaks of plague occurred in 1592-93, 1623, 1655, and 1675-76, and earlier quarantine stations had been set up on Corradino Heights and below the Del Monte Gate in Valletta. When Grand Master Lascaris appropriated the Barriera to commercial use (comp. Rte 1C), he moved the quarantine station to Bishop I. Cotoner altered the buildings in 1670; Carafa initiated new works in 1683; and Vilhena made improvements when he built the fort. By the mid-18C a disinfection station to accommodate 1000 transients had evolved, which dealt with crews, passengers, cargoes, and mail from all ships with foul bills of health arriving from the Levant. Ships with clean bills merely lay off Sa Maison for 18 days; the period of 'great quarantine' against bubonic plague was 80 days. The laws regarding avoidance of quarantine were strict, involving penalty of death. Mail was disinfected by cutting vertical slits and immersing letters in vinegar, then fumigated by sulphur or saltpetre. The system seems to have been effective, for the only major outbreak in later years occurred in 1813. Plague disappeared from Europe in 1841 and from the Near East soon afterwards, and modern prophylactic methods superseded strict quarantine. The lazaretto continued in use as an isolation hospital and during the First World War admitted wounded from the Dardanelles and sick from the Salonika campaigns. In 1922 it became a clearing house for refugees from Smyrna. During an outbreak of plague in Tunis in 1929 incoming mail was again fumigated in Malta, and the lazaretto was last used during an epidemic in 1936. Evacuated by the Health Department in 1940, the buildings served until 1949 as the base of a submarine flotilla. Opinion about their future is divided between restoration as a historic monument and demolition to make way for a yachting centre. (The medieval word 'lazaretto' is now spelled Lazzaretto when applied to the creek.)

Housed on the island just over the bridge is the Yachting Centre which manages the 260 berths for boats up to 50 metres in length. The berths which are for renting are placed in the following areas:

1. Torpedo Depot (Msida Creek)
2. White Hall Quay
3. Ta'Xbiex Quay
4. Lazzaretto Quay
5. Kalkara Quay in the Grand Harbour on the Vittoriosa side
6. Kalkara Quay in the Grand Harbour on the Bighi side

In the offices of the Yachting Centre are housed the Customs and Immigration Authorities who deal with the requirements of visiting yacht owners. On arrival yachts coming from abroad are advised after hoisting the International Code Flag "Q" (yellow flag) to proceed to Lazzaretto Creek in Marsamxett Harbour. A specific berth will be allotted after the necessary pratique has been issued.

Yachts registration book, as well as passports, covering all members of the crew and passengers are to be presented to the Customs Officer and to the Immigration Officer, who will call on the yacht as early as possible after arrival to enable the necessary practique to be issued. After compliance with the above no difficulty is normally encountered in the embarkation and disembarkation of passengers, nor for that matter for cruising around the islands.

Duty Free stores may be obtained after the appropriate forms are duly filled in. These stores will be loaded on the yacht under Customs supervision and sealed and may not be made use of within territorial waters. Before final departure from the Island, a Passenger/Crew list has to be drawn up on an appropriate form and presented to the Customs Duty Officer, whilst all passports are to be submitted to the Immigration Officer.

Yacht Harbour Approach

On entering the Yacht Marina Harbour (Marsamxett Harbour) to the west of the Grand Harbour Breakwater light, yachtsmen will easily see two direct boards at the east end of Manoel Island indicating the way to the Marina. This light should be rounded to starboard.

The amenities available at the yachting centre are as follows: Berths— Fees payable for berthing or mooring in a yachting centre in respect of any yacht, for every running metre or part thereof of overall length for every week or part thereof.

At the far end of the island by Fort Manoel, the Royal Malta Yacht Club founded in 1835, has its clubhouse with a membership of 1200, in

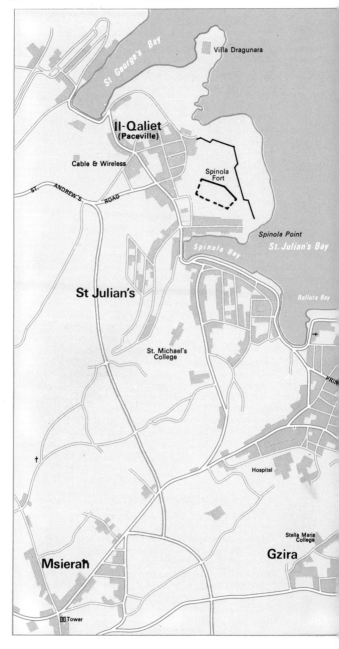

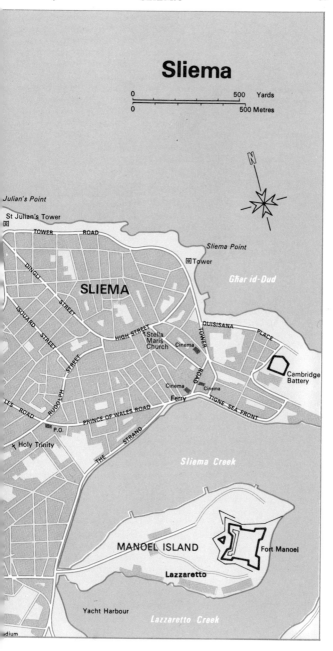

Sliema

all categories. Members of a recognised yacht club arriving in Malta can obtain temporary membership and use of the club facilities for up to three weeks for a fee of £M1.50. Overseas membership lasting not more than 6 months carries a fee of £M4.50. Full membership demands an entrance fee of £M12.60 and a fee of £M9 per annum. All enquiries to the RMYC Tel: 621839. At the end of September, beginning of October, the RMYC organises the famous Middle Sea Race around Sicily which is a main calendar event among yachtsmen who participate in ocean racing.

The *Manoel Island Yacht Yard* carries on the tradition of boat building and repair that goes back to the days of the Knights Hospitallers and today the yard has seven slipways capable of slipping vessels up to 62 metres in length of 500 tons displacement. Repair facilities in wood, steel and fibre glass hulls, engineering, electrical and electronics, textile, upholstery and canvas work are available. There is winter storage space for 300 yachts, 15 metres LOA and 2.15 metres draught. Head Office: Manoel Island Yacht Yard, Gzira, Malta. Cables: Slipway Malta. Telex: MW 211. Tel: 34453. Manoel Island also houses the "Anti-Pollution" regional offices of the Oil Combating Centre for the Mediterranean Sea, as well as the Supply and Distribution Centre for Oil Rigs in the Mediterranean. Beyond Manoel Island we skirt Sliema Creek, once a busy anchorage of the Royal Navy.

SLIEMA, the second biggest town in Malta (24,000 inhab.), occupies the large irregular peninsula that encloses Marsamxett Harbour on the N.W. On its S. shore the Strand runs along the sea wall of Sliema Creek, whereas, on the N., Tower Road faces the open sea above an extended rocky shore favoured for bathing. The Tigné peninsula runs S.E. from the larger one to end in Dragut Point.

The centre of Sliema may be placed where the Strand broadens between its junction with Prince of Wales Road and St Anne Square. Here is 'FERRY' bus terminus (though a regular ferry to Valletta no longer plies). TOWER ROAD, where at No. 9 Edward Lear stayed in 1865-66, crosses the base of the Tigné Peninsula, the greater part of which is inaccessible; within the military bounds is *Fort Tigné,* built at the order of Emmanuel de Rohan by the Chevalier Tigné in 1792 on the site of the siege headquarters of Dragut.

The principal attraction of Sliema is the coastal drive or walk from Għar-id-Dud Square, where Tower Road meets Quisisana Place, to St Julian's and St George's Bay. Beyond *St Julian's Tower,* one of De Redin's defensive outposts, a fashionable promenade affords pleasant views across St Julian's Bay. Main St., **St Julian's,** turns an abrupt corner to round BALLUTA BAY. Here we meet the farther end of Prince of Wales Road (named for its inaugurator in 1862), which crosses the peninsula as two long hills. At SPINOLA BAY, with a fishing community, is the Spinola terminus of the Sliema buses. Hence the road crosses inland of *Paceville,* a district where the erection of the Hilton Hotel stands on the site of the former Fort Spinola and dominates the development of a hitherto neglected stretch of coast. At the top of the hill, beyond the walled garden of the Spinola Palace (1688), St Andrew's Road bears left for St Paul's Bay (Rte 10A), while we continue by St George's Road past the Telemalta Corporation Offices. To the right a by-road leads to the *Dragonara Palace,* a sumptuous classical villa now transformed into a casino. Sad to relate its beauty and proportions have recently been distorted by gigantic neon lettering erected for commercial reasons. Adm 50c every day for roulette, baccarat, black-jack, etc.; restaurant. Our road ends at **St George's Bay,** commanded on the far side by the former St George's Barracks, built of local stone with graceful arcades and balustrades.

3 ˉ TOUR OF THE HARBOURS

The visitor should take one of the available tours of the harbours (2 hrs.). The main interest is now in the seaward view of the historical defences, the busy kaleidoscope of maritime activity that used to characterize the many creeks being now largely a nostalgic memory. The occasional visits of foreign navies and summer calls by cruise ships can greatly heighten the atmosphere. A commentary is provided during the voyage and only an identification of the principal points of interests is given below in the order of normal sailing. Most of the buildings are described in detail in Rtes 1, 2 and 4.

Boat tours turn s. across *Sliema Creek* towards MANOEL ISLAND, headquarters of a submarine flotilla in the Second World War. The star-shaped angle towers of *Fort Manoel* rise behind the rocky shore. Farther round the water laps the graceful arcades of the deserted *Lazaretto.* Yachts now line both shores of the creek that once spelt quarantined isolation to ships from the Levant. *Msida Creek* and *Pietà Creek,* where patrol boats of the Malta Land Force have their anchorage, are separated by Gwardamanġa Hill, crowned by St Luke's Hospital and the villa once occupied by Queen Elizabeth II.

We now cruise out through the deeper open anchorage of MARSAMXETT HARBOUR beneath the fortifications first of Floriana and then of Valletta. The spire of the anglican *Cathedral* along with the dome of the new Carmelite Church stands high above the cliff-like walls. To round *Fort St Elmo,* from the sea a formidable defence work, we briefly emerge into the open sea, then through the small boat passage in the breakwater enter ****Grand Harbour.** The damage done by the suicidal Italian attack of 1941 is still prominent.

We range the E. defences of Valletta, above which in succession slide past the *Sacred Infirmary* of the Knights, *Lower Barracca Gardens,* with the classical temple that is Sir Alexander Ball's memorial, and *Upper Barracca Gardens.* At water level are the attractive wharves of the Marina, the *Custom House* conspicuously graceful among the 17-18C store houses. The dome of *Ta Liesse* immediately draws the eye. The knightly wharves continue below the E. defences of Floriana, followed by the berths of the daily passenger ships to Syracuse and of other cruising liners. *Marsa Creek* has commercial moorings and modern warehouses.

We turn back along the indented E. shore of Grand Harbour. *Corradino Heights* rise to the right above partly derelict remains of the coaling and oiling facilities that once served the Mediterranean fleet. The floating dock was built in Bombay and towed through the Suez Canal to replace an earlier one sunk by Italian aircraft in 1942. FRENCH CREEK, with the entrances to four graving docks, once rang to the noise of the repair shops of the Royal Navy. Now merchant repairs and conversions are effected. The famous vedette carved with an eye and an

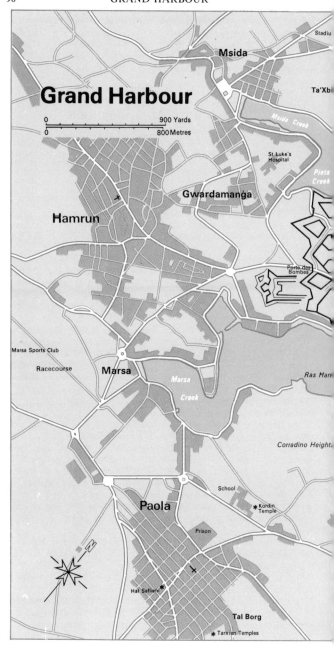

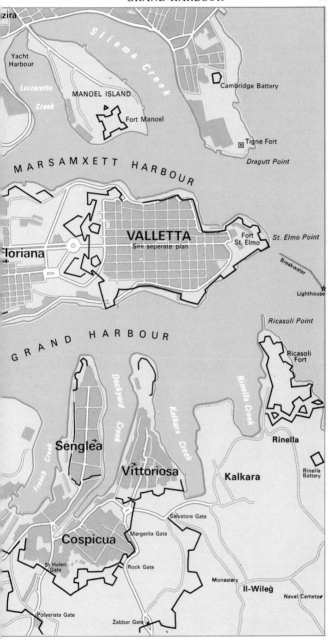

ear is prominent, symbolically watching and listening for the enemy fleet, as we round the peninsula of *Senglea* into DOCKYARD CREEK. Behind rise the cramped streets of Cospicua. *Fort St Angelo* on the point of Vittoriosa flies the admiral's pennant and proudly turns an impregnable face to the water. Between its base and the Senglea vedette stretched the great chain of the Siege.

Kalkara Creek and *Rinella Creek* are separated by Mt Salvator, the modest height on which the former *Bighi Hospital,* now a state school, displays its elegant classical façade. In this section of the harbour large tankers are generally moored off the storage tanks that partly occupy the derelict defence works of *Fort Ricasoli.* Fort St Elmo rises again over the bows as the steamer recrosses the bar for the return to Marsamxett.

4   THE THREE CITIES

We take the main road out of Valletta and, beyond the Port des Bombes descend to Mile End and take the l. fork for Marsa, where the Hamrun Road (Rte 8) leaves our road by an overpass. We fork l. and follow the main road which leaves Hamrun on our r. In the centre of the road stands the national emblem, a monument of a dgħaisa resting under a motif sun with a prickly pear shrub and winnowing fork and shovel beside it. Soon after leaving Marsa Sports Ground on our r. the dual regional road ascends to the new Marsa roundabout. We continue on the main road to Paola and at the second roundabout can be seen a Turkish and Jewish cemetery off to the right. Two roundabouts after the cemetery we take the route for Bormla (Cospicua). Passing the Technical School on the l. we come up to the next roundabout and cross over, taking the road en route for Zabbar until we come to Hompesch Arch (1798) where we cross over and make a wide curve towards the north and leave Zabbar (on the r.) to approach the Cotonera Lines.

The THREE CITIES, all older in foundation than Valletta, were renamed after the Great Siege. They comprise Vittoriosa (Birgù), Senglea (L-Isla) and Cospicua (Bormla). Throughout the 17C, in the face of a series of threatened and attempted invasions, their defences were strengthened. The Floriana outworks (Rte 1B) were barely started when Marculano da Firenzuola, summoned to review the defence works in 1638, warned that an enemy investing the hill of St Margherita, just E. of Vittoriosa, would command the entrance to Grand Harbour and be able to blockade the three cities. To incorporate both the hill and Cospicua, the **Margherita Lines,** designed by Firenzuola, were begun forthwith and three of the planned six bastions shortly finished. The remainder was not completed until 1716-36. In 1641 the Turks ravaged Gozo and effected a brief landing in Malta itself; there was a further scare in 1645. When Candia fell in 1669, invasion again seemed imminent. Nicholas Cotoner invited Maurizio Valperga to complete the works with a more comprehensive scheme. The **Cotonera Lines,** consisting of a semicircular ring of eight bastions and two demi bastions, with a circumference of three miles and capable of sheltering 40,000 people with their livestock, were constructed in 1670-80. Owing to lack of funds the ravelins which should have guarded each curtain were never built. Much costly repair work was effected in the first half of the 19C, but as early as 1831 some bastions were in civil hands as dwellings.

Between massive bastions rises the ŻABBAR GATE, round which traffic now passes through arches pierced in the curtain wall. The gate bears an inscription recording the gift of the works by Cotoner. Beneath its great arch the iron bars that held the doors are still in place.

The space between the outer (Cotonera) and inner (Margherita) fortifications is
adapted to various uses; though possessing its full quota of 'eyesores', it is of
considerable interest to the student of military architecture and in parts not
without a certain charm. The most interesting points can be explored on foot in 1-2
hrs and the road within the walls, though poor in the s. section, is negotiable by car.

Just within the gate we turn right into St Edward's St. between a new
estate on the left and *St Edward's College,* a boys' boarding school on St
James's Bastion, and overlooks (l.) the buildings of *De La Salle College,*
the boys' school of the Christian Brothers. It then skirts an attractive
little cemetery, planted with cypresses. St Louis Bastion, behind,
preserves its rampart walk (view). Beyond St Saviour's Bastion the road
joins the Kalkara road (comp. below).

Returning to the Żabbar Gate we take Cotonera Road towards the
Rock Gate entrance to **Cospicua** below the grim disused mass of *Verdala
Barracks* (1853). This gate is little used since the modern Silver Jubilee
Road skirts the inner defences to join St Edward's St. at the entrance to
Vittoriosa (see below). If we turn left outside Rock Gate, taking the road
which winds beneath high walls under the Margherita Bastion, we
emerge in a plantation of trees below the old married quarters on St
Nicholas Bastion. Beyond, a minor road from Fgura enters the lines by
the new *Polverista Gate,* its upper part for many years in popular
occupation. From it Blessed Virgin St. leads through the Margherita
Lines into Cospicua proper.

The road between the defences continues past St John Bastion and *Valperga
Bastion* (view of Docks) to descend to Għajn Dwieli Road (comp. p. 98).

We enter Cospicua by *St Helen Gate,* whence New St. leads directly to
the central Gavino Gulia Square, outside the s. gate of the Dockyard. A
good view of No. 1 Dock is obtained from the steps ascending to the
parish church of the *Immaculate Conception.* The greater part of
Cospicua is comprised of narrow streets and alleys rising in steps. St
Theresa's St. skirts the hill along the dockyard wall to reach the modern
St Margaret's Square. The bus terminus outside Vittoriosa. *St
Margherita's Convent* is prominent to the right.

VITTORIOSA occupies the narrowing peninsula between Dockyard
and Kalkara Creeks that ends in the Fortress of St Angelo. In medieval
times, as *il Borgo del Castello,* or in Maltese **Birgu,** it was the principal
centre of population on Grand Harbour, while the creek to the s. was the
Port of Galleys of the Arabs. During the Sicilian régime it was the seat of
the governor and until 1436 it shared with Mdina the ecclesiastical
division of the island into two parishes. The Knights made it their
residence in 1530. As in Rhodes they equipped themselves with a
headquarters, or Auberge, for each Langue; but monastic seclusion in a
Collachium (or inner city) was abandoned, though at least four of the
auberges formed a compact central group. The city was dubbed
Vittoriosa after the raising of the Great Siege, but the Knights moved to
Valletta. Though the town suffered grievously in the Second World
War, it retains some monuments from the period of the Order.

During the *Great Siege* of 1565, after the fall of St Elmo, the Turks turned all
their forces against Birgu and Senglea. The two peninsulas and the harbour
between were fortified as an entity. Across the harbour mouth was extended the
great chain expressly forged in Venice. The inland defensive works opposed two

VALLETTA

GRAND   HARBOUR

Fort St. Angelo

N

Dockyard Creek

Corradino Heights

French Creek

VICTORY STREET

MARINA STREET

SENGLEA

ST. LAWRENCE STREET

6

VICTORY SQ.

1

VITTORIOSA

School

St Michael's Bastion

St John's Cav.

ST MARGARET'S SQUARE

ST THERESA'S ST.

Margerita Gate

COSPICUA

P.O.

GAVINO GULIA SQUARE

Ghajn Dwieli

Valperga Bastion

St Helen Gate

Verdala Barracks (ruined)

Re... Ga...

Margerita   Lines

St John's Bastion

Poiverista Gate

Cotonera   Lines

St Nicholas Bastion

St Clement Bastion

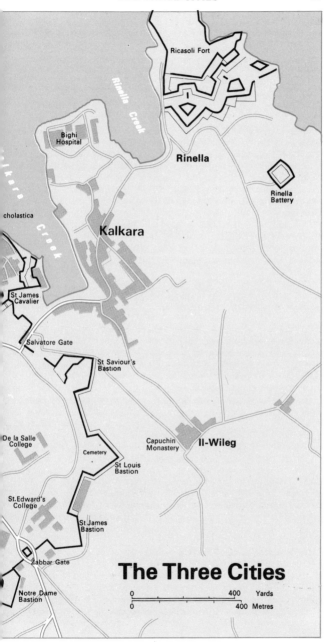

Ricasoli Fort

Rinella Creek

Bighi
Hospital

Rinella

Rinella
Battery

Kalkara Creek

cholastica

Kalkara

St James
Cavalier

Salvatore Gate

St Saviour's
Bastion

De la Salle
College

Capuchin
Monastery

Il-Wileg

Cemetery

St Louis
Bastion

St.Edward's
College

St James
Bastion

Zabbar Gate

Notre Dame
Bastion

The Three Cities

| 0 | | 400 | Yards |
| 0 | | 400 | Metres |

short fronts towards the mainland and rapid communication between the two was assured by a bridge of boats. Just after St Elmo fell a small relief force from Sicily—the 'piccolo soccorso'—had successfully reached Birgu under cover of a sea mist. The first attacks in July fell upon the s. shore of Senglea (L-Isla) where the Turks were engaged by Maltese swimmers on the improvised palisades. Hassem, viceroy of Algiers and Dragut's son-in-law, next led a land assault while his lieutenant Candelissa attacked from Marsa with a fleet dragged overland from Marsamxett. A squadron attempting to land Janissaries near the chain was blown out of the water by St Angelo's guns. The later attacks of August fell mainly against Birgu, where efforts were made by mining and with siege towers to invest the Castile bastion. At no time did the Knights retire to St Angelo, nor were the archives or the sacred relics in the conventual church taken to safety.

The present entrance by car to Vittoriosa is by the lowest Vittoriosa Gate. On foot, however, it is more interesting to take Couvre Porte Road, a little further up, pass through the *Advanced Gate* (1722), with attractive sculptured trophies of arms, and, making a dog's leg through the *Couvre Porte* (1723) and the *Vittoriosa Gate* (1727), enter across the moat. The moat itself is approachable by steps and prettily laid out as the Coronation Garden between *St John's Cavalier* and *St James's Cavalier.*

In the one way Main Gate St. stands the **Inquisitor's Palace** (Pl. 1), or *Palazzo del Sant' Uffizio,* built towards the end of the 16C round the interior court belonging to the Castellania (1530). The palace has recently been restored and opened to the public (adm. see p. 49; ring bell).

The Inquisition, or Holy Office, the papal instrument for the suppression of heresy, was established in Malta in 1562, though the first inquisitor seems not to have arrived until after the Great Siege. The office was abolished by the French in 1798. In the 19C the building was used as officers' quarters.

The audience and residential rooms have been furnished with pictures and pieces of no great merit that do not belong to the building; but the timber ceilings are notable, and the coasts-of-arms of various inquisitors that decorate the rooms include two who became pope: Fabio Chigi (1599-1661; Alexander VII) and Antonio Pignatelli (1615-89; Innocent XII). Beneath are the prisons.

From the irregular VICTORY SQUARE, farther on, Britannia St. leads to a group of buildings dating from before 1565. On the left the *Auberge of France* (Pl. 2), with a portal by Bart. Genga, faces Mistral St., where in succession on the left stand the *Auberge of Provence and Auvergne* (Pl. 3), Sir Oliver Starkey's House, and the *Auberge of England* (Pl. 4). In North St., farther on, is the *Auberge of Castile* (Pl. 5). A convent of Benedictine nuns occupies the first *Hospital of the Knights;* their church of *St Scholastica* has an altarpiece by Preti. The town walls, behind the convent, command Kalkara Creek. Old Prison St. ends by the ancient *Granaries* in steps that descend to the *Auberge of Italy* (Pl. 6). We return along St Lawrence St. which runs the full length of the town, but is cut off from Dockyard Creek by the high wall surrounding the naval purlieus.

St Lawrence, founded in the days of Roger of Sicily, and taken over by the Knights as their conventual church in 1530-71, was almost completely rebuilt to the designs of Lor. Gafà in 1691. The dome was ruined in 1942. The treasury contains a silver processional cross (carried round the streets on 10 Aug.) and relics brought from Rhodes. The *Oratory of St Joseph,* in the little square outside the N. door, preserves the hat and sword worn by La Vallette at the victory ceremonies in 1565.

A little to one side of the façade, steps lead down to the waterfront here unencumbered since the Marine Gate and part of the curtain were destroyed by a powder explosion in 1806. To the right is the main gate (no adm.; but comp. below) to Fort St Angelo. Just within, but better seen from the Senglea waterfront, is the monumental *Steam Bakery,* designed for the fleet by Scamp, with a clock tower inspired by that of Rennie's Victualling Yard at Devonport. The building was damaged in the bombing.

*Fort St Angelo, perhaps the symbol par excellence of the island's history, headquarters of the defending garrison throughout both sieges. Visitors are not permitted to explore on their own but guided tours are available (information from Tourist Office). The main entrance is reached from Dockyard Creek (comp. above), but on open days the best approach is by dgħajsa from Valletta.

History. A pagan temple occupied the site probably from Phoenician times and its Roman successor may have survived until, in the 9C, the Saracens built their first castle here. Count Roger built a small church dedicated to the B.V.M. in 1090. By 1274 there was a small church of Sant'Angelo in castro exteriore and another dedicated to Santa Maria in the castrum interius. The name St Angelo may derive from Angelo de Melfi who held the islands as his fief in 1352-53. The castle passed in 1430 to the de Nava family, who built a palace within the citadel and added the chapel of St Anne. In 1530 the Grand Master made it his residence, and here in 1531 during his absence in Mdina the Turkish slaves mutinied. Four 16C grand masters were originally buried in the crypt of St Anne: de l'Isle Adam, del Ponte, de Homedes, and Claude de la Sengle. The fortress bore the brunt of the Turkish attack after the fall of St Elmo during the Great Siege. The Grand Master moved out in 1571 and St Angelo had a governor. La Cassière was imprisoned here after his deposition for rashly attempting to curb the licentious behaviour of his Knights. The fortress was repaired and altered in 1687-90 by Don Carlos Grunenberg.

Under British rule the fortress became the headquarters of the commandant of the garrison, until in 1912 the Admiralty took it over as *H.M.S. Egmont* to replace the old base ship of the Mediterranean fleet (Hibernia, renamed Egmont 1904) which had been moored at its foot. As headquarters of the C-in-C. Mediterranean, the fort became *H.M.S. St Angelo* in 1933, and in 1935 the chapel of St Anne, which had been used as a store since 1798, was rededicated as the ship's chapel. Damage was done by sixty-nine direct hits in the bombing of 1940-43, when the slave tunnels were enlarged and used.

Senglea, approached from Gavino Gulia Square by Mons. Panzavecchia St., suffered badly in the war and has few monuments of note. It was fortified by Claude de la Sengle in 1554. Fort St Michael, scene of fierce defence in 1565, was dismantled in 1922 and the stone used for a school. Marina St. affords the best view of Dockyard Creek. On Isola Point a small *Public Garden* on the ramparts affords the finest **Views* of Valletta and of Grand Harbour. At the end is a celebrated vedette decorated with sculptured reliefs of an eye and an ear. Below are traces of the attachments of the Great Chain that guarded the harbour in 1565.

Malta drydocks currently operate 5 graving docks, the largest of which, No 4, can accommodate vessels of up to 110,000 deadweight tons. The drydocks also operate a modern tank cleaning installation which is situated at Ricasoli near the entrance to Grand Harbour. The first dock was opened in 1858. After 1865 the Royal Navy took over French Creek, the mercantile installations of which were moved to Marsa. The arrangements are in some ways reminiscent of those at Devonport, though the architecture is less distinguished. The Dockyard is completely isolated by a boundary wall, within which a separate complex of roads is approached through guarded gates. Connection between Dockyard Creek and French Creek is made by two tunnels through the base of Senglea under Panzavecchia St., and the complex includes the whole of *Corradino Heights,* where the principal depots were situated. Fortifications were erected in 1875. On the other side of French Creek by the Corradino Heights China Dock is being built with help from the Government of China. This dock will be capable of taking ships up to 300,000 tons and is expected to become operational in early 1979.

The most direct return to Paola or Valletta is by GĦAIN DWIELI ROAD which passes through the Valperga Bastion by a tunnel. At the top of the hill Cospicua St. continues into Paola, while Kordin St. (r.) leads directly into Paola Hill above Marsa Creek. The scanty remains of the Copper Age *Kordin Temple* are in the grounds of the prominent Technical School (key from Archaeology Museum, Valletta).

A new road linking the three cities, Senglea, Cospicua and Vittoriosa will be completed in the Spring of 1979.

THE N.E. QUARTER OF THE ISLAND. From the Salvatore Gate outside Vittoriosa a short descent brings us to **Kalkara.** KALKARA CREEK, once called English Creek when it was the anchorage for galleys of the langue of England, is now no more than a haven for dgħajsas, which are often to be seen beached for repair below the horn work of Castile. Rnella St. crosses the steep little peninsula of BIGHI, once occupied by the **Royal Naval Hospital,** and now a state school whose classical proportions make such an attractive contribution to the view from Valletta. The central building began its existence as the villa of Giovanni Bichi, grand prior of Capua, who retired to the then bare Mt. Salvatore from his position as Master of the Galleys. Both Napoleon and Nelson used the villa as a military hospital. The edifice was completed with the flanking wings c. 1840 by Gaetano Xerri.

Rounding Rinella Creek we turn a sharp bend, leaving to the left *Fort Ricasoli,* now derelict and partly occupied for oil storage. The fort, which derives name from Fra Giov. Fr. Ricasoli who paid for it, was designed by Valperga and begun in 1670 to replace a tower of 1629. During the siege a Turkish battery had occupied the point. The fort was the scene in 1807 of the mutiny of 'Froburg's Levy', when the mutineers blew up the powder magazine. In 1821 great breaches were made by the great storm of 8 February.

Behind Kalkara are the Capuchin monastery of Il Wileġ and a Naval Cemetery, from which narrow lanes wind through smallholdings above a fortified coast to *Marsaskala* (Rte 5).

5   VALLETTA TO ŻEJTUN AND MARSAXLOKK

Hal Saflieni, Tarxien, Tas Silġ

Leaving Floriana we take the main Marsa road which leaves both Hamrun and later the racecourse on the r. We follow the signposts and at the roundabout by the Industrial Estate we see in front of us on a hill the attractive Victorian gothic chapel (1869) of the Addolorata Cemetery. Its memorial tombs, shrines, and chapels have the architectural elaboration familiar in Italy. We continue on to the next roundabout and follow the signpost to Paola, and by Paola Hill leave the Kordin Prison on our l.

PAOLA or **Pawla,** a growing residential town (11,500 inhab.) with broad streets on a grid plan, is situated little more than a mile from the civil port and dockyard. It has a number of developing light industries and its s.e. extremities extend to the village of Tarxien (comp. below). From the square in front of the modern church of Christ the King we continue s. and leave the Tarxien road on our left. In Burials St. (r.) is the *Hal Saflieni Hypogeum, the most remarkable of Malta's prehistoric monuments. A labyrinthine subterranean sanctuary, discovered by accident in 1902 by workmen digging a well, it was cleared and systematically explored by Sir Themistocles Zammit. The modern entrance building contains show-cases of objects found during the excavations. The Hypogeum was essentially a vase burial ground which grew gradually and became more and more elaborate. It was in use during the whole of the Copper Age. The finely carved inner halls were almost certainly used for ceremonial purposes as well as burial (hence the elaborate decoration and imitations of the temple architecture). There was apparently some kind of megalithic building which stood in front of the original entrance.

The Hypogeum into which we descend by a modern spiral staircase is on several levels. The uppermost level may have been natural caves which first suggested occupation, but the lower levels were hewn out and fashioned with the most sophisticated architectural features. Most striking are the main hall and the so-called 'holy of holies', both given concave façades simulating trilithon doorways, windows, and corbelled vaults; the oracle room with an echo chamber of impressively supernatural effect; and a deep chamber approached by an interrupted flight of steps with possibly sinister implication. Some chambers have remnants of decoration in red or black pigments, including what is believed to be the outline of a bull, and incised representations of hands.

From the Hypogeum the quickest way on foot to the Tarxien temples (500 metres) is to turn back towards the church; Sammat St., the second turning on the right, leads directly to Old Temples St.

TARXIEN (8,000 inhab.) an agricultural village of narrow streets and tiny alleys, is famous for its **Temples**, excavated by Sir T. Zammit in 1914-19. Until the exploration of Skorba in 1961-63 Tarxien remained the only major megalithic monument in Malta to receive detailed publication after systematic digging. Though the largest and the most developed of the prehistoric remains in the islands, the Tarxien group of temples is less immediately striking than Ħaġar Qim (Rte 7) with its restored façade or Ġgantija with its more open position. Tarxien comprises three temples of different date but basically similar plan; as each later edifice was completed, the earlier structures became subordinate parts of the new. Presumably space was the requirement since the archaeological evidence proves that the whole complex continued in use until its common end. Some of the more important features (altars, etc.) have been removed to Valletta museum and replaced by replicas.

We approach the latest or **Third Temple** from a semicircular forecourt. The main entrance is marked by a huge convex threshold (Pl. A); the façade walls are now represented only by fallen fragments extending for c. 15½ metres to either side, though its former extent is clear. To the right the façade ends in a square structure (Pl. B); a huge stone block has six conical pits cut deeply in its surface and a large number of small stone balls were found in heaps near by. Possibly some form of divination by numbers was involved. The numerous large stone balls visible at many points were used as rollers in the transport of stone blocks.

Within the entrance a passage, paved with a single block, opens into a paved square space (Pl. C) surrounded by stone benches decorated in relief with spiral patterns. In the centre a circular patch of burnt floor shows the location of a sacrificial fire. Near by a stone basin with pitted decoration probably held ritual water. On the right stands an elaborate altar and in the apse behind are the remains of a colossal draped stone idol (originals, see p. 69). Here also were found, stratified above the Copper Age remains, and separated from them by about 1 m. of sterile sand, the cinerary urns and burial offerings of the Tarxien Cemetery people (see pp. 18). On the left, by a secondary altar with relief carving, a narrow entrance opens into an apsidal chamber (Pl. D), much ruined, where were found sections of a frieze (copies in situ near floor level). The many niches found in the temple contained half-burnt bones, horns, or skulls or oxen, sheep, goats, and pigs, the same animals as are depicted in stone.

The main passage leads to the inner shrine where a huge decorated block fronts a platform supporting a framed trilithon (Pl. E). The apse to the left has a floor of torba and a small shrine flanked by pitted slabs.

To the right a triangular space (architecturally a seemingly clumsy link) brings us to the imposing entrance to the **Second Temple.** Its main passage (Pl. F) is paved and the wall blocks are pierced with holes where doors were attached by rope or leather hinges and secured by bars. We reach another paved square (Pl. G) with a circular hearth, perhaps the most suggestive part of the remains. Large apses open to either side and the whole should be imagined with a domed roof, which probably collapsed after an earthquake. In the w. apse is a monolithic stone bowl, restored after damage by vandals in 1925. The E. apse (Pl. H) leads to the First Temple (comp. below); off its s. side opens a room decorated with relief slabs of two bulls and a sow suckling piglets.

The INNER APSES of the Second Temple were probably reserved to initiates or the priesthood since passage is impeded by an elaborately decorated slab. Beyond, a corridor extends between stone benches. These support screens carved with spiral ornament on a pitted background with traces of red paint. To right and left apses of especially well fitting upright slabs flank a central space with a hearth (Pl. J) similar to that in the Third Temple only smaller. A stone water basin stands in the left apse; between it and the wall was found the great terracotta bowl now in the museum at Valletta. A further fine threshold leads into the final pair of apses, where that to the left (Pl. K) preserves one of the curved stones that formed the base of the dome.

Returning to the main elliptical space (comp. above) we ascend two steps to the **First Temple,** altered when the second temple was added. A secret stair (Pl. L), to the left, fashioned in the reduced w. apse, by-passed this entrance. The innermost room (Pl. M) has the remains of a small chamber from which an 'oracle' spoke through a concealed hole in the wall.

Enormous blocks remain of the boundary wall that once enclosed the temple group.

A road runs s.e. from Tarxien to the crossroads of *Bir id-Deheb,* where it turns left.—8½ km. **ŻEJTUN,** an old agricultural village (10,000 inhab.), an early parish established before 1436, was formerly

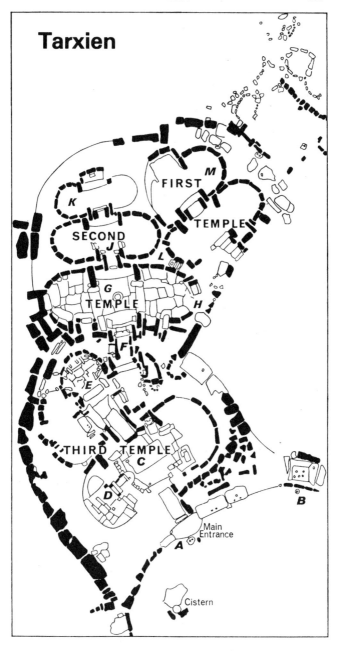

the administrative centre of the s.e. corner of the island. It was sacked in a Turkish raid of 1614. Our Lady of Mercy St. and its narrow continuations lead to the centre, an irregular square in the shadow of the parish church. Dedicated to *St Catherine,* this was begun by Gafà in 1692 and has the usual solidity of his work, the horizontal line being emphasized all round the building by massive cornices, while the vertical line is also strongly marked by superimposed buttresses, of Doric inspiration below and Ionic above. The dome is perhaps the most elegant part of the composition. St Gregory's St. leads s.e. to the old parish church of **St Gregory,** rebuilt in 1492 and enlarged after the arrival of the Knights with a massive but unfisnished transeptal (east end), surmounted by a low dome set upon a drum.

The simple façade was embellished with a Renaissance portal and a bellcot in the mid 16C. The tiny nave, of four bays, is buttressed externally, an unusual feature in a Maltese church. The original church is all but swamped by the Knights' transept, whose corner pilasters rise from a plinth but are left in the air at an unfisnished roof level. Secret passages containing the skeletal remains of more than eighty people have recently been discovered in the wall thickness of the north transeptal extension.

From Żejtun a road leads e. in 5 km. to Marsaskala (comp. below). On foot we may shorten the journey by branching left after 2 km. passing the little church of *Tal Ingrau* (or *Ta' Ingraw; 1597*).

Beyond Bir id-Deheb the road divides and we take the left branch (to the right, see Rte 6), shortly joining a narrow by-road leading directly from Żejtun.—9½ km. **Marsaxlokk,** or *Marsascirocco,* on the e. arm of the bay of the same name, is the largest fishing village (1500 inhab.) of the island. The huge bay offers the easiest sheltered landing; here both Piali in 1565 and Napoleon in 1798 disembarked their forces.

From Marsaxlokk to Marsaskala is a rural walk of 5 km. A by-road runs e. from behind the sea-front to Tas Silġ (1 km.) where, on a hill next to a Carmelite monastery, Italian excavators in 1963-72 uncovered a Punico-Roman temple. Vases dedicated to Tanit and Hera and a Punic inscription in stone to Astarte suggest that this is the celebrated *Sanctuary of Juno* plundered by Verres (as Cicero records). In 1966 remains of a Christian baptistery were found. To the s.e. a long peninsula runs out to Delimara Point.—Tracks continue e. of Tas Silġ battery to *Xrobb il-Għaġin* (2½ km.), a headland on the base of which are vestiges of a Copper Age temple.

Hence a track leads round *St Thomas Bay* to join the by-road from Żejtun (comp. above) just e. of the unusual *Mamo Tower* (17C), built on a saltire plan with a circular central chamber.—5¼ km. **Marsaskala,** on a narrow sheltered inlet, is another fishing settlement. In the bay a small Turkish force came ashore in 1614 and ravaged Żejtun, after which *St Thomas Tower* was erected on the headland to the s. to guard the landfall.

From Marsaskala we may return by an uninteresting road in a shallow valley via (3 km.) **Żabbar,** a town (10,000) which grew up in the 17C after the danger from piratical raids had diminished. It has a little Church Museum adjoining the Sanctuary of the Virgin of Graces. From Żabbar via Paola to (10½ km.) Valletta, see Rte 4.

6 VALLETTA TO BIRŻEBBUĠA AND KALAFRANA

Għar Dalam

We quit Valletta as in Rte 5 and take the new road by-passing Paola.—7¼ km. *Bir id-Deheb* crossroads, see Rte 5. Leaving on our left the road to Marsaxlokk, we continue s. with the valley of Wied Dalam on our right.

9½ km. **Għar Dalam.** The entrance (signposted) is on the right of the road (adm. see. p. 49). We pass through the little museum and descend a long path to the cave. The natural CAVE. running into the lower Coralline limestone for 215 metres at right angles to the Wied, was worn by the action of water. Traces of stalagmites and stalactites are visible. The floor of the cave, when excavated in 1865 and 1892, proved to consist of five well-defined layers. At the bottom were a metre of sterile clay; above this a metre of bones, tusks and teeth, mostly of dwarf elephant and hippopotamus, welded into a solid mass by the action of water dripping through the limestone. Above this again, in 1½ metres of red earth, were discovered bones and antlers of deer. The top layers, respectively 38 cms. and 23 cms. in depth, represented detritus of the Neolithic and Bronze ages, and of the period since Phoenician times. The large number of animal remains is explained most plausibly by the theory that the cave became a swallow-hole, trapping both dead carcases and live animals. Restored skeletons of some of the species found are displayed in the *Museum,* together with bones from some 7000 animals. These seem to be all of European type, similar to those of the Pleistocene era identified in Sicily, suggesting that Malta may once have been joined to Europe but never to Africa.

From the cave mouth we look across the stony valley. On the opposing spur, but neither readily accessible nor very illuminating, are a Roman villa site, the remains of a Bronze Age village, and the megalithic temple known as *Borġ in-Nadur* after the name of the locality. Partially cleared in 1881, the area was properly excavated by Dr Margaret Murray in 1922-27. At the point where the main road touches the coast there are traces of 'cart ruts' leading into the sea.—10½ km. *Birżebbuġa* stands on a headland separating St George's Bay from Pretty bay, two of the smaller inlets of the large landlocked Bay of Marsaxlokk. It has large oil storage facilities and a tanker jetty.—12 km. *Kalafrana,* near the w. entrance to the bay, was once an important R.A.F. flying-boat base.

From the bottom of the hill below Għar Dalam a new road (l.) continues E. round St George's Bay to *Fort St Lucian* (1610), now used for marine studies, then descends to *Marsaxlokk* (Rte 5).

From Kalafrana a minor road leads w. to *Żurrieq* (6½ km.; Rte 7), passing round the Fleet Air Arm airfield of *Hal Far.* Off the end of the s.e. runway 61½ metres above the shore is *Għar Hasan,* a large cave (torch necessary) said to have been used by a Saracen hiding to avoid expulsion in 1120.

An alternative return (approximately two and a half km. longer) may be made by turning w. at Bir id-Deheb to *Għaxaq,* whence a bus runs via *Gudja,* birthplace of Gerolamo Cassar (1520-86), the architect, to *Luqa* (Rte 7), and thence to Valletta. At Ix-XLEJLI, between Għaxaq and Gudja is the *Dorell Palace* (1770), Malta's finest 18C country house, where Bettina Muscati is said to have entertained in turn both Napoleon and Nelson. Midway between Gudja and Luqa, to the left of the road, stands the church of *St Mary Ta' Bir Miftuħ*, perhaps the best preserved of the later medieval parish churches. It is decorated with early 17C murals.

7   VALLETTA TO ŻURRIEQ AND QRENDI

Haġar Qim and Mnajdra

The road leaves the capital via *Marsa* (Rte 4), and skirts the S.E. corner of the Racecourse. Inside the track is the Polo Ground where Kipling's Maltese Cat had learned to be past pluperfect prestissimo player of the Game. We turn left. On the right is the huge hospital of St Vincent de Paule.—5¼ km. *Luqa* has given its name to the Airport which extends to the W. The church, begun in 1650, was almost destroyed in the Second World War. The altarpieces by Preti have been incorporated in the rebuilding. We leave the road to Gudja (Rte 6) on our left, and pass between Kirkop (l.) and Mqabba (r.; see below).

9 km. **Żurrieq,** a long village of 6600 inhab. The parish church of St Catherine, begun in 1634, has been several times modified. It has fine paintings by Mattia Preti, who lived in the village during the plague of 1675. In the adjacent garden are some remains of the Punic and medieval periods. The *Armeria,* a late 17C building, was used as an armoury during the grand-masterships of Pinto, Ximenes, and de Rohan, but became a private residence in 1784. The remains of a number of windmills date from the fifty years between 1674 and 1724 when the Order enjoyed a monopoly right to erect them. The village's most interesting monument is however the late medieval *Church of the Annunciation* which marks the site of the deserted settlement of the Millieri. It is an important example of 15C vernacular architecture and contains the finest wall paintings of the period. It is now held in trust by Malta's Conservation Society which undertook its restoration in 1974.

About 2 km. to the W. lies **Qrendi,** with 2000 inhabitants. A long main street runs almost N. and S. with the parish church off to the N.W. More interesting is the odd façade of *St Catherine Tat Torba* on the Mqabba road; plain blocks of masonry project from a recessed front to give a structural pattern. It was added in 1625 to an older nave. In Tower St. near St Saviour's, is the *Cavalier Tower,* the only tower on an octagonal plan in Malta. At the beginning of the Wied-iż-Żurrieq road is *Il-Maqluba* (literally 'turned upside down'), a depression 100 metres across and c. 50 metres deep, a geological vertical fault caused by the collapse of an underground cavern roof.

The return fare for the conveyance of persons from Wied-iż-Żurrieq to the Blue Grotto is as follows: 1 pers—50c, 2 pers—75c, 3 pers—87c5, 4 pers—£M1, 5 pers—£M1.12c5, 6 pers—£M1.25c, 7 pers—£M1.40c, 8 pers—£M1.50c. Trips are performed, weather permitting. Check first. Phone, 26721 or 26947.

The principal importance of Qrendi for the traveller lies in the two temple complexes situated to the S.W., the nearer of which is distant about 20 min. walk (signposts). **Haġar Qim,** the 'standing stones' were visible above the surface of the fields and suffered early and unscientific excavation in 1839. The restoration of the monumental façade, though somewhat crude at close range, gives from a distance a striking impression of the scale of Maltese megalithic architecture. Here were found many of the steatopygous figurines, or fat divinities, now in the museum at Valletta.

In internal arrangement Hağar Qim differs considerably from other temples on the islands in that additions of radiating oval rooms have been made to an existing trefoil plan without any attempt at preserving an overall trefoil arrangement. An ancillary entrance has been supplied at the back, another unusual feature. Otherwise, the same detailed characteristics are found: the rope holes, the roller stones, the apsidal arrangement, the pitted decoration, and the oracular chamber. The huge stone (7 m. x 3 m.) near the N.E. wall rivals that at Ġgantija as the largest quarried block in Malta.

From the temple a path descends W. On the left stands a watch tower of the Order of St John. Nearby is a monument erected to Sir Walter Congreve, governor in 1924-27, whose favourite spot this was. Ten kilometres offshore lies *Filfla*, an uninhabited islet that was used until recently as a gunnery and bombing target by the Royal Navy and Royal Air Force. It has a unique species of lizard. The path leads to another temple complex ½ km. away and some 38½ m. lower.

*Mnajdra, comprising two temples, is less exposed to the weather than Hağar Qim and better protected by an outer wall of hard coralline limestone. Although excavated early, it has suffered less alteration and in its remote and unspoiled setting is one of the most beautiful of Maltese prehistoric monuments. The temples, set with their axes at about 45 degrees, remain internally separate though having a common perimeter wall. The UPPER TEMPLE (r.) is entered by a port-hole slab within which an impressive vista opens through the inner entrance to the central apsidal shrine. To the left an inner room, also approached through a port-hole slab, has an altar.—The LOWER TEMPLE, probably older, has a more imposing entrance reached by steps. The usual trefoil plan has the addition of two rooms, fashioned either side of the short entrance passage between the façade and the main elliptical space. That to the right has a good torba floor, carved recesses and an oracular window. The main elliptical space has good pitted decoration and an exceptionally well-preserved trilithon entrance to the inner sanctuary.

In front of the temples and a little to the right is a small free-standing shrine. About 600 metres to the N.W. are six rock-hewn reservoirs of unknown date.

From Qrendi a short return may be made to the Zurrieq-Luqa road via *Mqabba* amid a vast area of quarries. Alternatively we may continue N.W. to Siğğiewi (Rte 8).

8   VALLETTA TO ŻEBBUĠ AND SIĠĠIEWI

From Floriana we take the middle road and just short of the centre of Ħamrun (comp. Rte 9) fork left.

4 km. **Qormi** (15,000 inhab.) used to be called *Casal Fornaro* because of its many bakeries. It has a confusing medieval lack of plan with very narrow streets, and suffered more than any place in the plague of 1813. The bus passes only through its southern outskirts. The High St. diverges to the right and has some notable carved doorways and balconies. The *Stagno Palace,* though in poor state, shows interesting details of its period (1589). The parish church of *St George* (1584) has a tall façade with prominent w. towers; the dome is possibly a later addition.

Nearly 1 km. beyond the town we join the modern road which, from Marsa, passes s. of the racecourse to bypass Qormi. At 5½ km. the direct road to Siġġiewi (comp. below) diverges left. Just beyond the turn a small chapel marks the track (r.) leading to *Tal-Ħlas,* a pretty church of 1690 amid the fields.—Just outside (7¼ km.) **Żebbuġ** the road divides into three, the left branch, the old Main St. passing through *De Rohan Arch* (1677) into a maze of narrow streets. Vehicles normally take the modern centre road, which enters the main square from the N. The town (8,000 inhab.), once famous for sail cloth made from locally grown cotton, is the birthplace of Dun Mikiel Xerri and Bp. F. X. Caruana, heroes of the revolt against the French, as well as of Dun Karm, the national poet, and Ant. Sciortino, the sculptor. *St Philip's,* the parish church, was built in 1599. The façade is given added apparent height since its span including the towers does not incorporate the aisles, neither are the aisle domes hidden by screens. The dome has a graceful lantern set upon an angular octagonal drum. Some of the houses beyond the E. end in Hospital Square are 350 years old.

The road continues to (9½ km.) **Siġġiewi,** an agricultural centre of 5,000 inhab. amid fertile fields and farms. The parish church of *St Nicholas,* designed by Lorenzo Gafà in 1675-93, is perhaps the most spectacularly Baroque work on the island, though the arcaded w. portico was not added until 1864. The dome, a later addition, rides proudly on a high drum, and the high vault allows a flood of light to illuminate the ornament of the interior. The fine palace of the secretary of the Holy Inquisition survives.

About 2½ km. to the w. in the locality called *Girgenti,* on the s. side of the Wied Ix-Xagri, stands the *Inquisitor's Summer Palace* (no adm.), a well-proportioned if fortress-like house built by Onorato Visconti (1625-27) in a delightful situation. The little chapel of St Charles Borromeo was added in 1760.—Rabat lies 5 km. N.w. of Siġġiewi.

Għar Lapsi, 'the cave of the Ascension', a fishing inlet, lies at the foot of the cliffs just w. of Mnajdra (Rte 7). Here there is a small beach and the modern road terminates in a car park by a restaurant. The place is a popular picnic and bathing centre with excellent views of the rocky islet of Filfla, an important breeding ground for the stormy petrel.

9 VALLETTA TO MDINA (RABAT)

Leaving Floriana, at Mile End (comp. Rte 4) we take the right fork to follow the long St Joseph's High Road through the busy centre of **Ħamrun.** Just N. of the central square on a site (Blata l-Bajda) once fortified against the French is a new student town. Here is preserved one of the locomotives of the former railway. In *Santa Venera,* now a w. extension of Ħamrun, we pass (r.) the 'Dar il-Lyuni', or *Casa Leoni,* a country villa built by Manoel de Vilhena in 1730. We cross the Birkirkara-Qormi road at Fleur de Lys roundabout and for the next 2½ km. follow the disused WIGNACOURT AQUEDUCT, built in 1610-14 to carry water to Valletta. It was originally 15 km. long.—At 6½ km. a by-road passes through its arches and crosses the bed of the former railway to reach **San Anton** (600 metres) now the principal residence of the President (no adm.). Built in 1625 as the country seat of Grand Master Antoine de Paule, who displeased the Inquisitor by the lavishness of his installation dinner here, it became the seat of the National Assembly from Feb. 1799 to the surrender of Valletta by the French in Sept. 1800. Here through the summer of 1810 ripened the romance of Lady Hester Stanhope and Michael Bruce, then on their way to the East. The attractive formal gardens are open free daily until sunset. San Anton forms part of Balzan (Rte 10B), though situated as near to

7 km. **Attard,** which lies just to the right of our road. Here the parish church of *St Mary,* built in 1613-16 by Tomasso Dingli, has been called the best Renaissance monument on the island. The large building, farther on (r.), is a hospital for mental diseases. We climb gently, then more steeply as the Qormi, Żebbuġ, and Siġġiewi roads come in one by one from the s., finally abruptly up Saqqajja Hill to the plateau (192 m.) on which stand (9½ km.) Rabat and Mdina.

MDINA, *the* city par excellence as its name implies, was named by the Saracens when they reduced the compass of Roman Melita and refortified the citadel. In 1427 Alfonso V of Aragon dubbed it *Notabile* and the Knights called it *Città Vecchia* to distinguish it from their new city, Valletta. All three names still have currency and the walled city (900 inhab.) which rides the surrounding fields like a proud battleship dominates with its characteristic skyline the greater part of the island. Within the walls cloistered calm and harmonious buildings invoke its noble past. Outside the walls to the s.w. extends the untidy town of **Rabat,** a centre (11,500 inhab.) of the cottage lace industry and the market town for the w. half of the island.

Bus Terminal and CAR PARK just outside the Main Gate.
Post Office, Museum Road.
History. *Melita,* the Roman capital of the island, occupied nearly the area now covered by Rabat until, after A.D. 870, the Saracens reduced its compass to that of the present citadel of Mdina. Here in 1090 Roger of Normandy was hailed as liberator of the island. Alfonso the Magnanimous honoured the city in recognition of its citizens' redemption of the island for 30,000 florins from the Sicilian viceroy. Sinam Pasha's attack in 1551 was beaten off while the Maltese cavalry under Sir Thomas Upton harried the invaders in the plain below. In 1565 the city organized sorties against the Turkish camp at Marsa and later inhibited attack by reinforcing the walls with women disguised as soldiers, a ruse which deceived the enemy. After 1570 the city lost population to Valletta though Grand Master Martin Garzes tried to prevent this by granting special privileges to those who stayed. Here in 1798 the people rose against the French occupation.

Buses terminate on the SAQQAJJA, a broad esplanade with a fountain on the edge of Rabat and just outside the walls of Mdina. The outer line of fortifications has disappeared beneath modern approach roads and the pleasant *Howard Gardens,* planted with palms, citrus trees and Mediterranean pine. The existing enceinte consists of an irregular quadrilateral of medieval walls with four projecting bastions added by G. M. de Redin in 1657-60. As we approach we have a good view of the s. wall with its three bastions, *San Pietro* on the w., *de Redin* in the centre, and *del Palazzo* on the right.

A narrow bridge crosses the dry moat (first dug by the Arabs and now planted or laid out with handball courts). The site of an earlier drawbridge may be located by the outline of the former entrance, now blocked, in the wall 20 m. to the right. The present **Main Gate,** erected in 1724, bears an inscription and the arms of Manoel de Vilhena. On the inside the arms of Antonio de Inguanez continue to be displayed in accordance (as the plaque states) with the order of Alfonso V. The present escutcheon was placed in 1886, the orginal having been removed by the French in 1798.

Within the gate we are in St Publius Square, a narrow space having on the left the *Torre dello Standardo,* anciently the gatehouse and now the police station. It dates from the early 16C; the Vilhena arms were added later. To the right the **Magisterial Palace,** built by Giov. Barbara for Vilhena, occupies three sides of an open courtyard which is closed by a screen and gateway. The principal façade has a fine doorway adorned with a portrait medallion of Vilhena in bronze. Used from 1860 until recently as the Connaught Hospital, the palace is now the *Museum of Natural History* which displays a large collection of birds, insects and fauna common to this environment.

We pass to the left of the massive walls enclosing the **Nunnery of St Benedict,** a closed order in strict seclusion whose members remain even after death in its own cemetery. The building dates from before 1418 but was altered in the 17C. On the corner as we reach Villegaignon St. is the little church of *St Agatha,* remodelled in 1694 to a design of Lorenzo Gafà, with an altarpiece by Gius. d'Arena. In the nunnery wall an inconspicuous portal marks the church of *St Peter,* which continues the dedication of the women's hospital that occupied the building before 1418. The altarpiece, Madonna with SS. Benedict, Peter, and Scholastica, is by Preti.

VILLEGAIGNON ST., the gently curving main street, is named after the French knight, Nicolas Durand de Villegagnon (c. 1510-71), who founded Nouvelle-Genève in Brazil (renamed after its capture by the Portuguese Rio de Janeiro) and (more relevantly) defended Mdina in 1551 against the Turkish attack. On the left a modern façade disguises the ancient *Casa Inguanez,* seat of the oldest Maltese family of title, created barons of Dyar-il-Bniet in 1350 and hereditary governors of Notabile before the arrival of the Knights. Here Alfonso V of Aragon stayed in 1432 and Alfonso XIII of Spain occupied the same room in 1927.

Facing the *Casa Testaferrata* (r.), seat of the Marquis of St Vincent Ferreri, are the 17C *Casa Viani* and the *House of Notary Bezzina,* once the offices of the Captain of the Rod. From its balcony the commander of the French garrison was thrown to his death on 2 September 1798 by citizens infuriated by his auctioning tapestries looted from the Carmelite church. Farther on (r.) stands the beautiful *Banca Giuratale,* or Municipal Palace, built in 1730 to the designs of François de Mondion by Vilhena when he appropriated the site of the older council house for his new palace (comp. above). It houses a girls' school.

The communes of Gozo and Malta were raised to municipal status by Roger of Normandy and has a form of local self-government. The Università (commune) had a consiglio populare, or council of jurats, elected from the heads of families. This had the right to appoint judges, to impose taxes, and to submit recommendations to the king. It reached its full development under Alfonso V. Among its officials were the Captain of the Rod, or chief magistrate, the four jurats, the Vice-Admiral, and the Secreto or tax-gatherer. In this building in Sept 1798, after the spontaneous uprising against the French commander the citizens declared a National Assembly and appointed Briffa to treat with Nelson against the French.

To the right opens ST PAUL'S SQUARE, its pleasing Renaissance harmony only disturbed by one unfortunate intrusion of Victorian gothic.

The **Cathedral,** dedicated to St Paul, a dignified Baroque building with a façade, almost austere for its period, was rebuilt by Lor. Gafà in 1697-1702 after its Norman predecessor had been ruined by an earthquake in 1693. It occupies, by tradition, the site of the villa where St Paul converted Publius, chief man of the island, after curing his father of a fever.

A church probably stood on the site from the 4C, and this or a successor was rebuilt by Roger de Hauteville soon after 1090. The church has always been the see of a bishop, though before 1530 the titular bishop frequently did not reside in the island. The see became an archbishopric in 1797 and a metropolitan province in 1944. The two brass cannons in front of the façade were restored to Mdina in 1888 from the Artillery Museum at Woolwich.

The INTERIOR, in the form of a Latin cross, has aisle chapels hung during festivals with crimson damask, giving a rich and unifying effect to the whole. The nave and aisles are paved with variegated heraldic slabs commemorating members of the chapter and dignitaries of the church— the ecclesiastical counterpart of the pavement in St John's in Valletta. The ceiling is frescoed with scenes from the life of St Paul by Vinc. and Ant. Manno (1794). The marble font inside the w. door was presented by Bp. Giacomo Valguarnera in 1495 and survived the earthquake intact; it comes from the Palermo workshop of Antonello Gagini. The *Sacristy,* approached from the 3rd chapel on the left, is closed by carved *Doors of Irish bog oak saved from the w. front of the Norman cathedral. Opposite the door a monument commemorates Bp. Caruana, one of the leaders of the revolt against the French in 1798.

In the *N. Transept* a painting by Mattia Preti depicts the miraculous appearance of St Paul during the Saracen raid of 1422. The *Chapel of the Blessed Sacrament,* to the N. of the chancel, has a possibly 12C Byzantine ikon of the Madonna inevitably attributed to St Luke.

On the chancel arch the two medallions of SS Peter and Paul are not paintings but mosaics. The ceremonial plate used on the high altar during the patronal festival includes silver candlesticks, and a set of statues of the Virgin and the Apostles which belonged to the conventual church of St John and are attributed to Cellini. The *Stalls,* of marquetry, date from 1481, but the panels were replaced in 1876 by Emmanuele Decelis. The *Apse,* reconstructed in 1681 to receive Mattia Preti's fresco

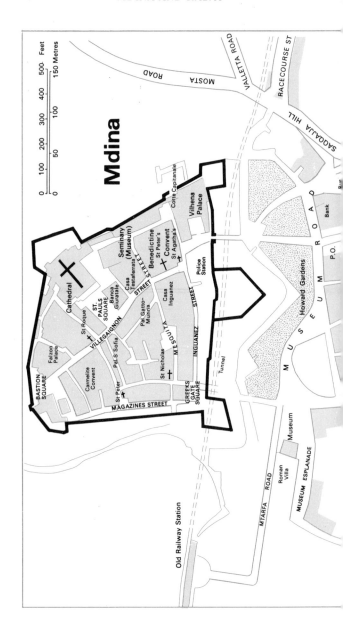

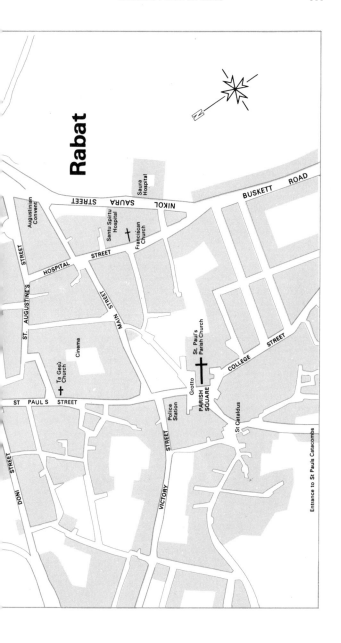

of the Shipwreck, withstood the earthquake.

The *Chapel of the Crucifix,* to the s. of the sanctuary, contains an interesting painting of St Paul, formerly the centre panel of a Siculo-Catalan polyptych forming the main altarpiece of the church. The crucifix is by Fra Innocenzo da Petralla (17C). In the *S. Aisle* is buried Lord Strickland, prime minister of Malta in 1927-32.

Abutting the s. transept stands the *Archbishop's Palace* (1733), the official residence as opposed to the Curia which is in Valletta.

The **Cathedral Museum,** deriving from a bequest of works of art by Count Marchesi in 1833, ranging over 400 years, is housed in the former *Seminary* opposite the s. door. Built in 1733 in a florid Baroque style of Sicilian inspiration, this building has a recessed centrepiece with a balcony supported in a seemingly casual manner by atlantes. The collections include the drawings, paintings and engravings of the original bequest, notably woodcuts by Dürer and engravings from them by Marcantonio Raimondi, engravings by Goya after Velasquez, and a drawing signed and dated 1581 by Luca Cambiaso. Among works that once adorned the cathedral are a Virgin at Prayer, by Sassoferrato, donated in 1687, panels from the 14C polyptych that once formed the main altarpiece (comp. above), and inlaid panels from the choir stalls by Parisio and Pierantonio Calatura of Catania. The vestments are specially interesting for fine specimens of ancient lace. The MSS include XI-XIIC antiphonals, homilies and a codex of the four gospels. A portable altar decorated with Byzantine enamel work is said to have been used in the galleys of the Order. The silver plate collection includes a superb set of fifteen statues made in Rome in 1748.

Recrossing the square, we return to Villegaignon St. The *Palazzo Santa Sofia,* on the left, displays a tablet of doubtful authenticity with the date 1233; the ground floor has, however, just claims to be the oldest building in Mdina. The upper floor was added in 1938. On the right is the tiny church of *St Roque,* popularly called 'Madonna tad-Dawl', which was removed here from the entrance gate during Vilhena's replanning operation. Almost opposite is the *Carmelite Church,* built after 1659 to the design of Fr. Sammut. The belfry was re-erected in 1857 after being thrown down the previous year by an earthquake. The confiscation of property from this church precipitated the revolt of 1798 against the French. The **Palazzo Falzon** (r.), often called the *Norman House,* originally a good example of the Siculo-Norman style which survived almost to the coming of the Knights. The building may not be earlier than c. 1495 and is said to be the house occupied by de L'Isle Adam after his first arrival in Malta. It is now a private museum which opens on Tuesdays and Fridays. The decorated double-lights were beautifully restored at the instance of Sir Harry Luke during his lieutenant governorship. The corner house (Beaulieu), beyond, incorporates part of the Benedictine nunnery of Santa Scholastica, founded here in 1496 and moved in 1604 to Vittoriosa.

BASTION SQUARE, the former firing-platform at the N. point of the city, though exposed to the full force of northerly gales, makes a wonderful vantage point from which the *View is one of the finest in Malta. On the opposing ridge, across the Hemsija Valley, stand the former David Bruce Military Hospital and the imposing cantonments of Mtarfa, given a focal point by a tall clock tower. Farther right in the middle distance the dome of Mosta rises from its hollow. In the distance, across the disused fighter airfield of Ta' Qali, stand out the fortifications round Grand Harbour. All round, amid a patchwork of stone-walled cultivated plots, the huge churches dominate their cream and golden villages. In every direction the distant sea borders the land. On a clear day Mt Etna's snow-capped crest in far off Sicily can be seen thrusting through its ring of cloud.

Bastions Street leads back shortly to the cathedral, passing *Casa Manduca.* Two other patrician houses (Depiro and Mifsud) are now linked by a bridge across the street and together house a girls' school. In the tiny square to the left is the entrance to a tunnel under De Redin Bastion by which the rebel Maltese forces penetrated the city in 1798.

The w. half of Mdina should be visited for its venerable calm and for the many exquisite details of its domestic architecture, such as window mouldings, brass knockers, and armorial bearings carved in high relief. Carmel St. leads to Magazines St. where the *Casa Isabella* has well-restored double lights. Behind the little chapel of *St Peter* (1617) runs a narrow lane where the medieval façades are lightened by delicate windows. From the church of *St Nicholas* it is possible to see through both the postern or *Gharreqin Gate* and the *Greek's Gate*, pierced in the oldest part of the walls, by which a road emerges through the moat into Rabat. MESQUITA ST., curving an unspoiled way across the city, is divided into three by the little Piazza Celsi and Villegaignon St. Off the centre section (l.) the *Gatto Murina Palace* has a fine 14C façade decorated with the lamprey motif of the family arms.

Turning right through the sombre St Paul's St. we reach a charming small square in front of the *Xara Palace*, formerly the seat of the Moscati-Parisio family and now a hotel. The foyer is adorned with vigorous bronzes by Sciortino. Opposite stands the *Corte Capitanale,* where figures of Mercy and Justice and the inscription 'Legibus et Armis' recall its former function of criminal court. Beneath there are still dungeons from an earlier building. It has for a long time shared the functions of the Vilhena Palace which it adjoins. The graceful loggia that closes the square in front of the E. rampart was the *Arengo* from which the town herald proclaimed the regulations of the Università or 'harangued' the citizens.

Quitting Mdina by either the main gate or Greeks Gate and recrossing Howard Gardens, we find ourselves in Museum Road. To the right is the **Roman Villa Museum,** a misnomer, for the remains on which it stands are those of a town house rather than a villa. During the excavations of 1881 a number of mosaic floors were uncovered. Busts and heads of various emperors, pottery and inscriptions are displayed beneath a restored peristyle.

We enter **RABAT** by St Paul's St. which, passing Ta Doni and Ta Gesù churches, leads directly to the parish church. **St Paul's,** given its present form at the end of the 17C, seems to have been remodelled in order better to combine the earlier parish church of 1575 with a chapel of St Publius erected in 1617. The latter had been a work of piety of Giovanni Beneguas, who came from Cordova to join the Knights but instead lived as a hermit in the GROTTO OF ST PAUL, a cave now beneath the church (open 2.30-4.30). This is locally venerated as either the 'dwelling' or the 'prison' of St Paul and credited with a miraculous propensity for staying the same size however much stone is removed from it.

Crossing an irregular square in front of the little chapel of St Cataldus, we take St Agatha's St. On the left is the entrance to **St Paul's Catacombs** (adm. see p. 49), an extensive system of passages and alcoves used as a burial place in the 4-5C. Farther on, to the right, are *St Agatha's Catacombs* (daily 9-12, 1-6), dedicated to a young girl who fled here from the persecutions of the Emp. Decius in Catania.

An avenue through St Paul's Churchyard leads into the narrow Main St. which we follow back to the Saqqajja. At the bottom of Saqqajja Hill the Siġġiewi road is known as Racecourse St. from the custom of racing horses and donkeys here on 29 June. The grandstand of the Grand Masters survives and the Mnarja races draw crowds from all over the island.

In St Augustine's St. the great *Augustinian Church*, designed by Cassar in 1571, has a gilded barrel vault. In Hospital St., to the left, adjacent to the Franciscan Convent, stands the former *Santo Spirito Hospital*, established before 1347 but no longer in use. Behind, in the main road, is the *Saura Hospital* of the Sisters of Charity, founded in 1667 and occupying a commanding situation on the edge of the town.

Buskett Road leads s.e. past St Dominic's Priory (16C). About a mile outside the town stands *Verdala Castle (no adm.), a summer palace designed for Grand Master Verdalle by Gerol. Cassar in 1586 in the form of a fortified medieval keep surrounded by a moat. Its halls and dungeons were used in 1812 to house French prisoners of war. Verdala, now used to accommodate visiting state dignitaries, is laid out with an elaborate garden and a 'Boschetto' of Aleppo pines and citrus trees. These shady *Buskett Gardens* (open daily) are a favourite retreat in summer.

A by-road turns w. to *Dingli,* the highest village on the island, situated a bare 1 km. from the tremendous *Cliffs that in this quarter drop 250 m. almost sheer into the sea. To the s.e. of Verdala, off a by-road to Siġġiewi, is Girgenti (Rte 8).

FROM RABAT TO MĠARR AND GĦAIN TUFFIEĦA, 9½ km. We take the Mosta road and in the Wied Ta l'Isperanza turn left. The road passes over the gentle *Falka Gap* and crosses a fertile valley.—6 km. *Zebbieħ*. At the police station is kept the key to the **Skorba Temples,** the scanty remains above ground excavated by David Trump in 1961-63. Here a temple of the usual trefoil plan has modifications of the Tarxien period; the complex was sacked and decayed before being used as a burial ground before the end of the Copper Age. The main discovery was of two superimposed hut settlements, characterized by the grey and red pottery wares which have taken the name of the site. These date from the 4M b.c. Nearly 2 km. to the w. in the village of **Mġarr** are the *Ta' Ħaġrat* temples, with similar remains.—9½ km. **Għain Tuffieħa** is a long sandy bay approached by a steep flight of steps. Non swimmers and children must only venture into the sea when it is calm as there are dangerous undercurrents in rough seas.

10   VALLETTA TO ST PAUL'S BAY AND MELLIEHA

A   By the Coast Road

St Paul's Bay and Mellieha are served by a wide range of buses out of Valletta. By car, after exploring the less populated regions in the west (Route 9) one can quickly cut across from Għain Tuffieħa to St. Paul's Bay. The quickest route from Valletta is to go to Msida and take the regional road. Behind St George's Bay we pass on our r. St Andrew's Barracks which extends to *Pembroke Fort* (1878), a defensive work that takes name from Lord Herbert, secretary for war in 1855. The steep hill (l.) crowned by *Madliena Fort* forms the N. end of the escarpment dividing the island (comp. below); a steep by-road climbs to Għargħur. Our road descends to the coast at 14 km. *Baħar iċ-Ċagħaq Bay* (14 km.), then crosses the fortified Qrejten Point on which stands Qalet Marku Tower.

The *Għallis Tower* on the next headland is accessible and typical of many defensive structures built by the Knights. We round SALINA BAY (*Salina Bay Hotel*), where salt pans have been worked since the early days of the Knights. By the farther entrance to the hotel is a redoubt and interesting remains of a *Fougasse,* effectively a mortar hewn from the living rock and designed to decimate any force attempting a landing. At the head of the bay the *Kennedy Memorial Grove,* designed by Joseph Spiteri (1966), commemorates with dignified simplicity the murdered American president. Off the track behind the grove are some scanty remains of *Tal-Qadi Temple.*

At 20 km. we join the road from Mosta, comp. below.—21 km. *St Paul's Bay.*

B   Via Mosta

From Valletta to *Msida,* see Rte 2. We keep straight on by Valley Road, passing (r.) an ancient wash-house, and rising gradually in the Msida Valley.—3¼ m. **Birkirkara,** an old-established village (17,500 inhab.) of narrow streets, extends mainly to the N. of our road. *St Helena's,* a youthful work of Dom. Cachia, was built in 1727-45 in a rich Baroque which has earned it the description of 'the finest parish church on the island'. Externally the façade, the aisle screens, and the entablature are notable, while within the frescoes are striking. The restored church of the Assumption (1617), designed by Vitt. Cassar, lies to the left of the main road near the old railway station. Beyond the centre of the town we bear right and pass through the N. part of (6½ km.) *Balzan.* At the edge of Birkirkara, a new sanctuary built by the Carmelite Fathers dominates the skyline. Here the parish church of the Annunciation (1669-95) has an unusual façade of Spanish inspiration. Down Three Churches Street leading off the main square, we come to three little churches grouped together. *St Roque,* built in 1593 during the plague. Next to it is the little *Church of the Annunciation,* a typical example of 15C ecclesiastical architecture in Malta, and beside this a third small church now *Ermina House* and private property. In front of this group is a little square with a stone cross on a tall pillar which may mark the site of an earlier cemetery.

To our l. lies the village of Lija one of the historic 'Three Villages' of Malta, the others are Balzan and Attard. In the main square is *St*

Saviour designed by Giovanni Barbara in 1694. Inside the rich painting of the vault, dome and semi-dome of the apse catches the eye. In St Saviour Street is the old parish church of Our Saviour built in the 16C. Just outside Lija in the exact geographical centre of the island is the *Church of Our Lady of Miracles* (Tal-Mirakli). It was rebuilt by the Grand Master Nicolas Cotoner. The Virgin and Child with St Peter and St Nicolas by Mattia Preti is the altarpiece.

Naxxar, an ancient village (4,500 inhab.) and a parish since 1436, is now isolated from the main routes across the island. From its commanding ridge the relief force of Ascanio de la Corna charged down on Mustapha's forces in the last battle of 8 Sept 1565. The modest dimensions and severe form of the parish church of *Our Lady of Victory* (1616) are disguised by an assertive façade, higher and wider than the nave, added with the aisles in 1912. The grounds of the *Palazzo Parisio* have been since 1960 the venue of the Malta International Fair.

From Naxxar minor roads descend in every direction, one to the N.W. passing through the Victoria Lines (comp. below) by the Naxxar Gap to Salina Bay (5 km.). The 55 bus goes N.E. to **Għargħur,** another high and isolated village (1700 inhab.), whence a winding road and steep descent joins the coast road beneath the Madliena Fort built to protect the eastern flank of the Victoria Lines. The parish Church of *St Bartholomew* designed by Tommaso Dingli in 1636 is by the bus terminus at Għargħur.

To the north of Naxxar some 500 metres is San Pawl Tat-Targa (Steps of St Paul). The 17C church *St Paul* on Naxxar ridge has a commanding view of the Burmarrad Plain. On this site, it is traditionally held that St Paul preached to the local people. Behind the church is a tower with its small balcony, built during the Knights' period by Cikko Gauci. Facing the church is another tower on one's left marked by a plaque Torri tal-Kaptan. It was built in 1558 and under the supervision of the Captain of the Maltese cavalry was used as a lookout over St Paul's Bay and Salina Bay. Within the tower can be seen the coat of arms of the Grandmasters La Vallette and Hompesch. A narrow pass road runs down to Salina Bay passing some of the most clearly marked cart tracks (see p. 23) and the Victoria Lines.

10 km. **Mosta** (8,000 inhab.;) is dominated by the huge *Dome of *St Mary's,* a landmark from many parts of the island. The church was built in 1833-60 in imitation of the Roman Pantheon to the designs of Giorgio Grognet de Vassé, and the dome was erected without the use of scaffolding by notching each course to the one below. It is claimed to be the third largest in the world, exceeded in size only by St Peter's, Rome and St Sophia, Istanbul.

In 1942 the dome was hit by three Axis bombs. Two bounced off and fell into the square without exploding and the third fell through and after hitting the interior wall twice, rolled across the floor during a crowded service without exploding. Not one person was hurt and the bomb is now kept in the vestry as a miraculous memento.

Mosta is a good starting-point for walks along the **Victoria Lines,** a series of forts (1875-80) with supporting works along the escarpment caused by the *Great Fault.* This natural feature has always provided a tempting defensive line with the result that the unprotected N.W., despite its greater fertility, has remained sparsely populated. Minor roads follow virtually the full length of the ridge, and these and paths nearer the edge afford a series of wonderful views of the indented coastline.

The NORTHERN END (Mosta to Għargħur, 5 km.) may be reached by taking the St Paul's Bay road (comp. below) and beyond the bridge turning right. Leaving Fort Mosta on the left we recross the Wied Ta l'Isperanza and follow the Lines across the *Naxxar Gap* to Għargħur. Here a by-road leads along the flank of Ġebel San Pietru to a signal station overlooking Salina Bay. The principal road winds round a rocky gully to *Fort Madliena* (comp. above).

The SOUTHERN END (Mosta to Baħrija, c. 10 km.), where the ridge is more elevated, is further from habitation. At the *Targa Gap* on the St Paul's Bay road a by-road follows the ridge, crossing the Mosta-Għain Tuffieħa road in the *Falka Gap.* A long steep hill climbs w., then divides round the crest of the ridge. *Id-Dwejra (210 m.), a commanding situation, affords magnificent views down to Għain Tuffieħa, and on the s. side looks across the *Chadwick Lakes,* a series of reservoirs in the Wied Tal-Qlejgħa, to Mtarfa. Beyònd the *Binġemma Gap* the road rises again to the *Nadur Tower* (242 m.), where there are good examples of prehistoric 'Cart-Tracks', then crosses the *Santi Gap.* This is here threaded by a road from Rabat, which descends N. past the remote and rocky *Gnejna Bay* to Għain Tuffieħa. To the s. of both of the roads that continue to the edge of the w. cliffs above Fom Ir-Riħ Bay lies *Baħrija,* a hamlet with a late Bronze age site.—On the return any of the roads branching off to the s. lead to Rabat.

We quit Mosta in a N.W. direction, cross Ta' l-Isperanza Valley by a bridge over the Wied il-Għasel, and descend abruptly through the *Targa Gap.* To the right Mosta Fort crowns an isolated rocky eminence; it is now a trade school. At the hamlet of (14 km.) *Bur Marrad* we meet a by-road descending from Naxxar just inland of Salina Bay. On the lower slopes of Ġebel Għawżara, 350 metres to the s.w., stands the little 17C church of *San Pawl Milqi.* Here Italian excavations since 1963 have uncovered remains of three previous churches on the site. Adjacent were rediscovered remains of a Roman villa first noted in 1879, which flourished from 1C B.C. to 4C A.D., and was latterly used for the manufacture of oil. A well-head inscribed 'PAULUS' and a graffito depicting a wrecked ship attest the early association with this area of the landfall of the apostle.

Keeping right at Wardija crossroads, we soon join (15¼ km.) the coast road (Rte 10A) half way between Salina Bay and St Paul's Bay. Here a by-road (r.) runs to the Qawra Tower, passing after another 1¼ km. some remains near the shore of St Paul's Bay of a neolithic *Temple,* generally known as that of Buġibba (comp. below).

19 km. **St Paul's Bay,** more correctly *San Pawl il-Baħar* (2750 inhab.), extends for a kilometre along the s. side of the bay from which the retreating forces of the Turks made a fighting re-embarkation in 1565. Its little harbour is guarded by the *Wignacourt Tower* (1610). Hardly a gap separates the houses from those of *Buġibba* to the E. Across the bay *St Paul's Islands,* really little more than rocks, are by tradition the site of the apostle's shipwreck in A.D. 60 (Acts xxviii, 7). The largest islet has the Maltese name of Selmunett and bears a statue of 1845.

Rounding the head of the bay we leave on our left a road through Pwales Valley to Għain Tuffieħa (4 km.; Rte 9). A short sharp hill takes the road over the E. end of Bajda Ridge. On the long steep climb up Mellieħa Ridge (154 m.) a by-road (r.) gives access to SELMUN PALACE, with its attached chapel. This castle-palace, built by Dom. Cachia in the 18C on a plan deriving from the Verdala palace, was once the property of the Monte di Redenzione, a charitable foundation founded by Father Rafael in 1607 to ransom Christian slaves from the Barbary coast.

21¼ km. **Mellieħa** (4,000 inhab.), occupying a dominating position on its ridge, was made a parish in 1436 but abandoned before 1530 owing to Corsair raids. Its present plan dates from the agricultural colonization of the mid 19C. The steep main street descends by corkscrew turns below the *Church*, which stands on a commanding spur above a rock-cut chapel of uncertain date.

In *Mellieħa Bay*, with a shallow sandy beach, the relieving force of the Sicilian viceroy landed on 6 Sept 1565. The road here is sometimes flooded in winter. *Marfa Ridge*, surmounted by another steep approach, is guarded by the *Red Tower* on which an inscription records its erection in 1649. The ridge commands a fine view across the S. Comino Channel to Gozo.

Along the ridge a road runs E., from which six parallel roads at regular intervals descend to the Channel, serving various batteries and redoubts. This curious geometrical road plan is not military in origin, however, but part of a scheme of agricultural colonization of the 1840s.

The main road descends to the landing stage at (25½ km.), *whence the ferry plies to Gozo.*

GOZO

GOZO, in Maltese **Għawdex,** the smaller main island of the Maltese group, is separated from Malta by a channel some 8 km. wide. Less fortified and less defensible, without a major harbour to serve as a base, it has remained a backwater, too close to have a distinct existence, suffering the sister island's misfortunes but rarely sharing her prosperity and never her political importance. Though the geological formation is the same, the outcrops are different, so that Gozo has a number of bare flat-topped hills rising above a more undulating landscape. The outcrops of blue clay are more extensive, making the land more fertile, and Gozo's chief rôle has been to supply agricultural produce to the more populous island. Though half the size of Malta, Gozo has only one tenth of the population. Fishing provides an alternative livelihood and, for the women, the making by hand of the exquisite lace for which both islands used to be famous. The Gozitans lead a serene and simple life, the survival of which depends on whether they are visited by those wanting relief from modern ways or those intent on introducing them. The principal attractions are the scenic walks. Gozo has been called, not entirely without justification, the 'Ireland' of Malta.

History. That *Gozo* has always had direct connection with Maltese culture is shown by the similarity of the Ggantija temples to those of Tarxien and Ħaġar Qim. In general the history of the two islands is indissolubly linked. But even as early as the Bronze Age pottery styles evolved with variations between the two islands. Both Malta and Gozo had municipal status under the Romans, and the cultural differences widened during the Saracen period when Gozo remained more largely Christian than Malta. The Sicilians granted both islands a Università (comp. p. 109) and there is no evidence that one was subservient to the other. In 1551 the Turks invaded Gozo and thousands of inhabitants were carried off into slavery after the garrison capitulated. The island was afterwards treated as a security risk, the office of Captain of the Rod (or Ħakem) abolished, and a governor appointed by the Grand Master. Gozo was attacked by the Turks for the last time in 1708.

Transport in Gozo—Almost all villages enjoy good road services to the main town and from the latter to Mġarr, the landing place. Bus services are not very frequent because the movement of population in Gozo is fairly minimal. There are plenty of taxis to take the visitor anywhere on the island. They are available at all times and even cheaper than on Malta. A booking office has been opened at Mġarr where tourists can get information from the Gozo Taxi Association on availability. Tel: 76543.

11   VALLETTA TO VICTORIA (RABAT)

A regular bus service from City Gate in Valletta connects with Ċirkewwa—Mġarr ferry (½ hr crossing) whence bus to Victoria. The ferry also takes a limited number of cars. It is also possible to hire a car at Mġarr. In winter, gales sometimes prevent the crossing. Day trips to Comino occur on a regular basis by cruise ships from The Strand, Sliema.

The bus follows the inland road through Attard (comp. Rte 10B) to *Ċirkewwa;* from Sliema it is shorter by private car to follow the coast road (Rte 10A). The steamer leaves from Ċirkewwa except in bad weather. We pass to the s. of **Comino,** on which *St Mary's Tower* (1618), built by Alof de Wignacourt, commands the South Comino Channel (Il-Fliegu ta' Malta). Here, off the s.E. coast of Comino, H.M.S. *Sultan* was wrecked in 1889.

COMINO, or *Kemmuna,* a rocky island (2½ sq. km.) of Upper Coralline limestone, supports less than 30 inhab. on scattered farms, but is frequented for its good bathing. Here, between 1285 and 1291 Abraham ben Samuel Abulafia, the Jewish sage from Saragossa, wrote his best known prophetic work. *Santa Marija Bay,* on the N. coast, above which stands the little church, has a fine sandy beach, while in the adjacent *San Niklaw Bay,* to the w., stands the Comino Hotel. The fractured s. coast, off which lies the uninhabited islet of *Comminotto* (Kemmunett), has a picturesque lagoon popular with underwater enthusiasts.

Landfall on Gozo is made at **Mġarr,** the principal harbour of the island, generally full of gaily painted small boats. The little port is dominated by Our Lady of Lourdes, a modern church in an alien Gothic style, from which there is a fine view across the strait. To the s.w. rises a steep promontory crowned by *Fort Chambray.* Designed in 1723 by De Tigné as a fortified township to replace the Castello, it was not built until 1749-60 when the cost was defrayed by Jacques François de Chambray, a French knight who had achieved fame as commander of the galleys. The interior was laid out in square plots on the pattern of Valletta, but few of the plots were taken up and a town never materialized. The fort put up an unavailing resistance to the French in 1798 and was garrisoned for a time by British troops. Today it only shelters a hospital.

The road climbs up the valley to *Għainsielem,* almost continuous with Mġarr, where a new church of huge proportions stands on a prominent spur. Beyond the village we pass Santa Ċilja Tower in an area cleared in twelve days in 1943 to make an airstrip for the invasion of Sicily. We cross the road coming from Qala (Rte 12) to *Xewkija* (2500 inhab.), which lies to our left. Here stands a huge new Rotunda church. The dome rivals Mosta and the church has been built mainly by voluntary village labour. To the right Xagħra is prominent on its ridge.

6 km. **VICTORIA** named for the diamond jubilee of 1897, or **Rabat** as it is still generally known, is the little 'capital' (5000 inhab.) of Gozo. Both in its inland fortified position and in its twofold composition of

citadel (Il-Kastell) and suburb, it resembles the old capital of Malta.

We enter by the broad Republic Street, passing (l.) *Rundle Gardens,* where the annual agricultural show is held on 14-15 August. Beyond the Commissioner's Residence and the Marsalforn turning, we enter the old part of the.town. On the left is the *Post Office.* IT-TOKK, the 'Main Square', with a monument to the fallen of the Second World War unveiled by Queen Elizabeth II, separates the citadel from the suburb. Here the former seat of the Government of Gozo sat in the *Banca Giuratale,* erected (1733) by Vilhena for the Università. From *St James's,* rebuilt in 1740, the crops are annually blest on the feast of St Mark (24 April).

The steep CASTLE HILL mounts (r.) to **Il-Kastell,** now entered by a broad modern archway, created since the Second World War. To the right is the old Entrance Gate adorned with a Roman inscription from a still earlier gate. From a confined piazza steps admit to the CATHEDRAL, designed by Lor. Gafà and built in 1697-1711. The church of the Assumption was raised to diocesan status in 1866. The three heraldic plums of Grand Master Perellos are prominent in its decoration. The font is of locally quarried alabaster. The trompe l'oeil painting in the dome is by Antonio Manuele. On the w. side of the square are the *Public Registry,* which before 1551 was the residence of the Ħakem of Gozo, and the *Law Courts,* erected by Wignacourt.

A small arch to the E. of the cathedral leads to the MUSEUM in the former Palazzo Bondi. On the ground floor are displayed agricultural implements and Roman remains from the island, among them a marble head of a boy and numerous amphorae recovered from a wrecked wine ship in Xlendi Bay. The upper floor, devoted to the prehistoric period, has finds from the excavations at Ġgantija, including objects connected with fertility rites, stone rollers, and pottery.

Turning right, we may reach the ramparts, which afford a marvellous *Panorama of the island. From this vantage-point the differences between the Gozo landscape and that of the sister island are very marked: from undulating fields rise sharp outcrops of rock on whose eroded tops ride the straggling villages. We pass the now disused *Prison* and come to a cavalier built by Alof de Wignacourt. A flight of steps mounts to the next rampart walk, commanding both the surrounding countryside and the ruined medieval buildings within the walls. Two Siculo-Norman houses survive in fair condition amid the encroaching prickly pear.

To XLENDI, 3¼ km. S. A steep hill descends into the narrow Xlendi Valley which ends in a pretty land-locked *Bay sheltering the fishing hamlet of **Xlendi.** A path round the S. side of the bay affords striking views of the vertical cliffs opposite, in which opens Carolina Cave. Underwater research has recently produced Roman remains from sunken galleys.

12   EXCURSIONS FROM VICTORIA

The bus services radiate from Rabat, but hardly anywhere on the island is out of reach of good walkers.

A   To the Ġgantija and Marsalforn

BY-ROADS, affording a pleasant walk of c. 6½ km., practicable by car.—Buses to *Marsalforn,* 3 or 4 times daily; more frequently to *Xagħra* (no connection between the two villages).

The uninteresting direct toad to Marsalforn (3 km.) descends in a long valley, dominated from the N. by Il-Mirzuk, a conical hill with a where a concrete statue of the Saviour was set in position by helicopter. The statue was destroyed recently by a thunderbolt and is being replaced by a new one made of fibre glass.

We take Republic Street and after 1 km. bear left and (2 km.) left again. On our left rises the irregular plateau on which stands the scattered village of **Xagħra,** the population of which (3,000 inhab.) is declining. Where the main road to the village starts to zigzag uphill (l.) we continue straight by a by-road that climbs between the plateau and the isolated hill of Nuffara (probably occupied in the Bronze Age). We arrive shortly at (3¼ km.) the **Ġgantija,** in some ways the most impressive of all the Maltese Copper age temples, though the protective fence detracts from its commanding situation. The monument was fully uncovered as early as 1827. The complex comprises two temples, the main one to the left with a subsidiary structure (smaller and later) to the right.

The FAÇADE is remarkably well preserved, with a huge threshold slab. The usual pivot holes, hinge holes, and bolt holes are prominent, and some of the blocks are adorned with spirals or pitted decoration. Most impressive are the majestic proportions of the perimeter wall constructed of header and stretcher stones of gigantic size.

A path across the fields, or Parisot Street, slightly longer, leads to the centre of the village, prominently marked by its *Church,* where a recumbent figure under a side altar (l.), recalls those of the Sicilian folk plays. Near the church two small limestone caverns (Għar ta' Ninu and Għar ta' Xerri), each opening from a private dwelling, show the usual stalactite formations.

A more direct return to Victoria may be made by Church Street and its continuation Steep Street. As Xagħra Road this way joins the main Marsalforn road just below its junction with Republic Street.

A difficult descend on foot may be made from the village to Ramla Bay, better reached from Nadur (comp. below).

The roads either side of Xaghra church join as another Racecourse Street, at the end of which the left fork begins the long descent (3 km.) towards Marsalforn. On the way there are pleasant views of the valley (l.) with the prominent Tas-Salvatur. On the ridge to the right wind pumps irrigate the fields.

Marsalforn, an attractive fishing village, borders a rocky bay in which a tiny harbour provides shelter from northerly gales. It is a popular summer resort of Maltese from the towns and abroad, but in winter many of its cottages turn a shuttered front to the sea.

A road passes salt pans on its course round the coast W. toward *Żebbug* (2½ km.) a village (1000 inhab.) occupying a steep and picturesque ridge (127 m.) running N. and s.

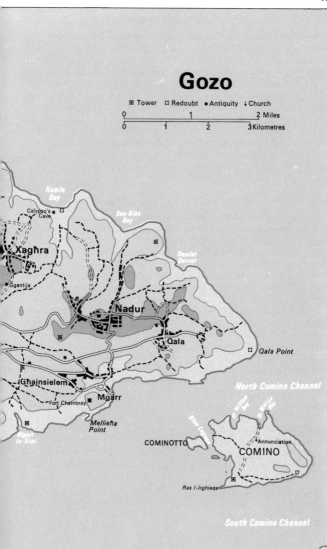

Gozo

⊞ Tower □ Redoubt ✳ Antiquity ⚲ Church

0   1   2 Miles
0   1   2   3 Kilometres

Ramla
Bay

Calypso's
Cave
San Blas
Bay

Xaghra

Damiet
Qorrot

✱ Ggantija

Nadur

Qala

Qala Point

Ghajnsielem

North Comino Channel

Fort Chambray

Mgarr

Il-Wilġa
Bay

St Marija
Bay

Mellieħa
Point

Mgarr
Ix-Xini

COMINOTTO

Blue Lagoon

Annunciation

COMINO

Ras I-Irghieqa

South Comino Channel

MALTA

B   To Nadur and Calypso's Cave

We take the same road but keep right at the second fork, climbing on to the ridge occupied by (5 km.) Nadur, a small town of 3,000 inhab. with a sumptuous Baroque church. To the N.E. in the 'Grove of Pomegranates' the quarry is disused that supplied stone for the crypt of Lutyens' Roman Catholic cathedral in Liverpool.

From the W. entrance to the town a by-road runs N. along the ridge, then descends into the Ramla valley. High above the sandy beach of Ramla Bay is *Calypso's Cave,* by tradition the Homeric spot where the Calypso bewitched Odysseus on his way home from the Trojan War.

Other tracks radiate from Nadur through orchards to *San Blas Bay,* and down the Daħlet Qorrot valley, while the road continues to *Qala,* also linked by road with Mġarr.

C   To San Lawrenz and Ta' Pinu

The western part of the island, distant from easy landing-places and with its approaches protected by the Kastell, suffered least from piratical incursions and its villages preserve more early buildings. The main road runs N.W., passing the turning for Ghasri and Zebbuġ.—At (2½ km.) a fork below the conical truncated hill of Ta Għammar (170 m.) a by-road diverges right to the imposing basilica of **Ta' Pinu,** erected in an eclectic style in 1920-31. It covers the medieval chapel where a local peasant woman heard the voice of the Virgin in 1883. Ex-votos attest various miraculous cures and escapes from misfortune. The church lies between Għammar and Għarb and c. 1 km. from either by track. About 550 m. farther along, the main road again divides. By the right branch we may reach (4 km.) *Għarb,* while the left branch continues W. to *San Lawrenz.*

A new road descends a steep hill to an area where a number of geological faults combine to make a series of splendid natural features. QALA DWERJA is an almost circular lagoon closed on the seaward side by *Fungus Rock.* The repellent plant which gives the rock its name was successfully dried for use by the Knights as a dressing for wounds and a remedy for dysentery. The plant was gathered by means of a primitive aerial ropeway and the approach guarded by a tower. Near by is *Tieqa Zerqa,* the 'window in the cliff', another natural rock formation. To the N. is *Il-Qawra,* an island sea to which water (and fishing boats in calm weather) can enter by a fissure in the rock. Its crystal waters make it attractive to swimmers.

Excavations at *Ras Il-Wardija,* on the S.W. promontory of the island, have uncovered a rock-cut Punic shrine with an altar on the seaward side.

INDEX

NOTE: Topographical names are printed in bold type; names of persons in italics; other entries in Roman type.